modern buffets

EDWARD G. LEONARD, CMC

Photography by John Ormond

WILEY

JOHN WILEY & SONS, INC

modern buffets

Blueprint for Success

Photo direction and design by Graham Walters

This book is printed on acid-free paper. ∞

Chapter 1 Opener: Picture Collection, New York Public Library, Astor, Lenox, and Tilden foundations.

For general information on our other products and services, or technical support, please contact our Customer Care Department within the United States at 800-762-2974, outside the United States at 317-572-3993 or fax 317-572-4002.

Wiley also publishes its books in a variety of electronic formats. Some content that appears in print may not be available in electronic books. For more information about Wiley products, visit our website at www.wiley.com.

Library of Congress Cataloging-in-Publication Data

ISBN: 978-0-470-48466-1

Printed in the United States of America

10   9   8   7   6   5   4   3   2   1

This book is dedicated to all the culinary students and apprentices who follow their dream, driven by the love of a simple thing called food. Teaching the craft of cookery is an art, the art of inspiring students who want to learn, stimulating their appetite for knowledge, and satisfying their hunger to excel.

◇◇◇◇◇◇◇◇◇◇◇◇

CONTENTS

RECIPE CONTENTS

FOREWORD

It is with great pleasure that I write this foreword for Chef Edward Leonard,CMC. And it is only fitting that it be for his grand book on buffets, as our relationship started while we were standing around the Grand Buffet at the Balsams Grand Resort Hotel in Dixville Notch, New Hampshire, almost 25 years ago. Our profession has taken us both all over the world since then, and we have shared the honor of representing the United States in the World Culinary Competition Arena. The ultimate prize for us both, however, has been the opportunity to work with young professionals from all over, trying to make a difference in their lives and encouraging them to realize their own goals.

A book such as this is long overdue, and we have Edward Leonard, CMC, to thank for sharing his expertise with us in *Modern Buffets: Blueprint for Success*. We have all seen horribly designed buffets, in regard to flow, eye appeal, temperature, elevations, and varieties, presented on plain, old tired-looking tables. Chefs may blame their lack of originality on budgetary restrictions, claiming they cannot afford to buy new equipment to improve the look of their buffets; they may also contend they don't have time to research newer, better options, or that their guests do not want anything different. Or it may be that chefs simply lack the motivation to improve their buffets.

Modern Buffets clearly demonstrates that there really are no excuses for poor buffet presentation. Relying on his many years as a professional chef, a master chef, and manager of the United States Culinary Olympic Team, Chef Leonard has created a blueprint that will ensure the success of your buffets. His professional roles—until recently, as the executive chef for a private country club—have demanded creativity on a daily basis, and it is based on those experiences that he brings to you fantastic recipes and design concepts sure to raise the standard in buffet presentation and preparation.

To me, however, the best part of *Modern Buffets: Blueprint for Success* is that it is inspiring—you will find inspiration in areas where you may not be looking. For example, I have always been a big breakfast fan, having grown up in a resort atmosphere. Yet many times breakfast menus are stagnant. That need not be the case anymore, for Chef Leonard develops contemporary ideas based on classical foundations. And that is only the beginning. You will find new ideas for lunch and dinner menus, for salads, finger foods, small plates, and so much more. He keeps no secrets here. Chef Leonard shares everything with you.

After reading this book, you, too, will know all the secrets. It is then up to you to execute, be inspired, and, in turn, become an inspiration. Happy cooking.

Chef Charles M. Carroll, CEC, AAC
River Oaks Country Club
Houston, Texas

PREFACE

What is the American buffet? Is there really such a thing as a quality buffet? These are just two of the questions I am frequently asked by chefs around the world, and that I have attempted to answer here in **Modern Buffets: Blueprint for Success**. In the past, U.S. cuisine and service style have often been misunderstood and, on occasion, criticized. Fortunately, times have changed; today we are regarded as leaders in many areas of the culinary arts—or at least can be said to rival our global counterparts.

I have traveled extensively as part of my profession—working with quality chefs across the globe, cooking, and giving lectures on cuisine. I have experienced the bounty of food to the fullest, and in all aspects of the culinary craft. In my more than 22 years of experience, I have seen buffets evolve dramatically, from the "grand buffets" in the great hotels to culinary shows to the all-you-can-eat extravaganzas that favor quantity over quality. I remember staying up nights, painstakingly creating truffle paintings to decorate a beautiful ham coated with chaud-froid. I recall, too, the days of carving vegetable flowers, making salt-dough centerpieces, or crafting small sculptures destined to be the attractions on a large silver tray of culinary artistry.

As cuisine has progressed, so has the structure of the buffet and the types of food displayed on it and served from it. Today, the buffet menu and presentation follow the same path as the modern à la carte menu: streamlined, fresh food displayed in a modern manner, with a focus on smaller portions and a variety of flavor infusions. The modern buffet is many things to many people, from the less expensive, all-you-can-eat to the most elegant and expensive brunch and dinner offerings.

In **Modern Buffets** I will challenge you to think, to reexamine your approach to providing buffet cuisine to your guests. I hope you will come away energized, and inspired to add your own ideas and personal touches to your buffet menus.

To the Student

The modern buffet is more elegant and streamlined than its predecessors, offering quality food that has been prepared in batches and presented to the customer fresh and full of flavor. Buffet spaces and counters are now being designed by world-class architects for top-ranked venues. Buffet chefs cook in front of their guests, generating excitement and interest in the new concepts they develop. Service vessels made of many materials, nonskirted tables, and small plates are all features of today's buffet world. Even ice carvings have come a long way. Gone are the days when they were just decoration; they are now incorporated as part of the buffet service.

Modern Buffets is intended as a guide, to help you develop buffets that are right for you, your guests, as well as the venue, event, and occasion. Along the way, I offer my own philosophy regarding buffet service, starting with some history on this style of food service, insights about its current status, and thoughts on its future. My goal is to encourage you to approach buffets in a new way and to consider innovative ideas for preparing and presenting timeless classics that, due to customer acceptance over time, are here to stay.

To Instructors and Professional Chefs

The modern buffet is versatile; it can be scaled to serve any-size event and be designed to provide an experience equal to any à la carte meal. Regardless of the setting, a modern buffet can add an elegant dimension to any mealtime, any event, be it breakfast, lunch, or dinner, an upscale reception, or a casual coffee break. You can think of a buffet cuisine as a stew, composed of many ingredients, which, even though presented together, do not lose their identity as distinct dishes.

Modern Buffets is meant to excite you, to inspire you to keep our craft moving forward, making advancements. The recipes here offer both new dishes and modern interpretations of classic recipes with contemporary presentations.

This book has something to teach culinary artists at all levels—chefs, cooks, and students—about buffet service and menus, while offering encouragement to be creative, to come away with new food concepts and design ideas. As a food professional, you can use it to review what you already know, yet be motivated to move the culinary arts forward in a positive direction.

ORGANIZATION OF THE BOOK

Modern Buffets is organized to provide an understanding of the buffet's evolution and introduce new ways of preparing and presenting buffet dishes. Included throughout the text are 11 buffet blueprint drawings to help you visualize innovative approaches to setting up buffets. The book concludes with setup and display suggestions that will move your buffets from the mundane to the modern.

Chapter 1: *Evolution of Buffets* provides a brief history of buffets and their styles, and how modern buffets have evolved from them.

Chapter 2: *Sensational Breakfasts* demonstrates new concepts and reconceived favorites for the most important meal of the day.

Chapter 3: *Lunch for All Occasions* features a new take on lunch items and their presentation for buffet service, and showcases the elegance of old favorites.

Chapter 4: *Composition of Flavorful Salads* shows how to spice up and present an ever-growing list of menu items that keep buffet service fresh.

Chapter 5: *Dinners with Flair* presents classic dinner recipes with new twists and service ideas, with a focus on the simple and elegant art of presenting buffet dinner food in a modern way.

Chapter 6: *Finger Foods* features small-bite items that are big on flavor and whose presentation will enhance any buffet reception.

Chapter 7: *From the Glass* offers another take on small bites; here, they are presented in glassware for a unique way to display and layer flavors.

Chapter 8: *Small Plates, Big Flavors* showcases small-plate dining to promote the concept of tasting as a way for guests to sample new foods and food combinations.

Chapter 9: *The Art and Taste of Pastry* introduces a modern approach to pastries, one based on a classical foundation, for an elegant and flavorful display that will ensure your pastry buffet is the talk of any event.

Chapter 10: *Classic Buffets Made Elegant* highlights items that have stood the test of time, presented here with a contemporary look.

Chapter 11: *Dine-Around Buffets* is all about the state of the art in the buffet world: stand-alone stations that take a fresh approach to buffet dining, one that both benefits the guest and has advantages for your operation.

Chapter 12: *Working the Buffet* treats the buffet as the canvas on which to display your offerings. It focuses on color, texture, and height, and includes a section on functional and decorative ice sculptures.

Chapter 13: *Menus: Concepts and Accentuating Ideas* is a food-for-thought chapter, meant to get your creative juices going.

Appendix A: *From the Chef's Pantry* contains foundation recipes you can use to build or enhance your buffet dishes.

Appendix B: *Where to Buy What You See* lists some of the purveyors that have led the way for modern buffet presentation, and that are represented in this book.

Additional Resources

An **Instructor's Manual** with **Test Bank** (978-0-470-49088-4) is available for qualified adopters of **Modern Buffets**. It can be downloaded for free from the book's companion web site, www.wiley.com/college/leonard. This companion web site provides readers with additional resources and enables instructors to download the electronic files for the Instructor's Manual and Test Bank.

It is my hope you come away from reading **Modern Buffets: Blueprint for Success** not just with new recipes and buffet design concepts, but also a broader, more contemporary way of thinking about and cooking for buffet cuisine. Please enjoy the book. Let it fire your passion for food, even as it gives you a fresh outlook on the presentation of buffets.

Chef Edward G. Leonard, CMC
Passionate Cook
Certified Master Chef
Culinary Olympic Champion

ACKNOWLEDGMENTS

This book was produced from my love of and passion for the art of food display, with purpose and with flavor. It's important that I thank and recognize those who make a difference.

I first want to express my appreciation to Lloyd Abanilla and artist Bobby Castillo, of Seagull Glass Works, Inc., and their families, for producing the finest glassware display products I've ever seen. Their commitment to the craft—and, more importantly, to chefs—is unrivaled. I have known and worked with them for over six years and, in that time, have seen my buffets and visions come alive on the canvas they give me. They take glass to a new level. The national culinary teams in Asia, too, owe a measure of their success to the hard work and dedication of these master craftspeople.

I want to thank the following protégés for their passion with this project and their assistance throughout the process: Chefs Jonathan Moosmiller (the lead project chef), Joseph Albertelli (an extraordinary ice carver), and Pastry Chefs Marianna Gambino and Cara Larocca. Your futures are indeed bright and it was my honor to have trained and worked with each of you.

My Chief Steward, Jean St. Hillare, who is responsible for setting up every one of our buffets and keeping the canvas, tables, and all else in shipshape order. And to my photographers and partners in many crimes, Graham Walters and John Ormond, many thanks. Finally, to my core, talented kitchen brigade, Jason, Veronica, Charles, Mike, Allison, Dave, Danny, Han, Justin, and CJ, thank you for all your help, and may your careers be all you want them to be.

Last, but far from least, much thanks to those who inspire, support, offer friendship, and push me to be my best: Chefs Brad Barnes, CMC, Joachim Buchner, CMC, Daniel Scannell, CMC, Shawn Hanlin, CEC, Kirk Bachmann, CEC, and a passionate cook and business leader Brian Williams—you would love his salmon!

CHAPTER ONE

EVOLUTION OF BUFFETS

The term *buffet* can be used to describe either a large sideboard or credenza that contains china dishes, special tableware, and crystal, or a room or table set to serve refreshments, feasts, and receptions. When *buffet* is used to refer to a set food table, guests are free to move about the room where the table is well positioned so they may easily select what entices them. At most buffets, guests help themselves to the food they have chosen; at butler-style buffets, they are served.

Deciding on the way to display a buffet requires knowledge of specific rules, which range from knowing how to choose the appropriate vessels for serving food to how to coordinate the décor so that it enhances the buffet table and/or its theme. Buffet food must look and smell appetizing and evince natural colors

and flavorful aromas. Likewise, the many platters, dishes, and food displays must be appealing to the eye. They should be garnished to look stunning, yet never at the expense of taste and freshness. Though simple in concept, in practice this task is not always easy to accomplish, which is why some people perceive buffets as poor quality. The French, regarded by many as the founders of and leaders in ornamental grand buffets, have always paid close attention to both the quality and substance of the ingredients used to create buffet or presentation food. In particular, they avoid using overworked, disharmonious foods paired with artistic arrangements that, together, make the food appear less appetizing and negatively affect its taste.

BUFFETS IN HISTORY

The ancient Egyptians crouched, by themselves or in pairs, before small tables to eat, each with an individual portion of food in front of him or her; pharaohs, and high priests ate lying down. The elite of Egypt naturally ate a greater variety and much higher quality of food than the poor, who typically dined on bread and local vegetables.

Greek servants were perhaps the first to adopt something similar to the modern buffet; but rather than laying the plates on tables at which the guests were seated, they first set the tables with food and place settings, paying no attention to arrangement, then carried them in and positioned them in front of the sofas on which guests were reclining. During the Roman Republic (509–27 BCE), serving procedures were similar to those in Greece. Often, lavish feasts, attractions, and elaborate displays were intended as much to amuse and amaze

guests as to feed them. This early style of dining showed that even then the experience and the wow factor was important to the guest.

Starting in the sixth century, tableware was set on boards, which rested on trestles that could be taken outside during pleasant weather. When Charlemagne (742–814) and his paladins sat down to eat after a battle, they wanted everything to be perfect. Tablecloths made their first appearance at this time, and were lengthy enough so that guests could also use them as napkins. Spoons and knives were provided for each individual (forks did not come into widespread use until the 1500s). Carvers were equipped with huge silver or metal-plated prongs with handles that could be inserted into the food to brace it for carving. Wealthy people ate from silver, and sometimes gold, tableware, whereas the poor ate out of

wooden or ceramic bowls. During this era, many people served themselves from large common platters of food and placed their portions on large pieces of bread.

Shortly thereafter, the luxury of Europe was nurtured by Venetian cultural standards, and later augmented during the Crusades (1095–1291). The Venetians, long skilled at making money, had found easier ways to do so than confronting the perilous seas. Now they profited from the land, by trading grains and, above all, salt from the sea. The eating habits of the Crusaders were, however, rather dismal and unappealing. Far away from their home countries, with supplies hard to come by, they ransacked and devastated the lands they traveled through and conquered. Royalty and military commanders ate their meals from large pots, similar to fish kettles, carried by their followers.

During the Renaissance, after 1300, the fork began making its appearance in every Italian court as a habitual utensil for guests. The early fork was usually made up of two or three prongs, often extending from a finely etched handle made of precious metal. At about the same time, the napkin came into popular use, and was frequently changed throughout the course of a meal. It was quite large, and designed to fit around one's neck so as to protect frilled collars and fine clothing.

Massive carved tables soon replaced the boards set on trestles of the medieval period (fifth to fifteenth centuries). At the same time, the cuisine improved, and an effort was made to formalize table manners, evident in the publication of treatises on etiquette. However, early forms of rustic buffets still featured courses served at random and in large quantities, seemingly with no rhyme or reason as to the assortment of flavors and types of foods being served. Each guest would take as much as he or she pleased of whatever was within reach,

regardless of the combinations. That said, the art of table serving and setting had become a subject of study and debate, with writings starting to emerge on this new concept.

By the sixteenth century, gala luncheons were being served, yet the tables were set more or less as in the past, filled to capacity with food, plates, and silverware. Glasses were not included; guests had to request them, as needed. It was not until the eighteenth century that each guest was provided with a complete set of silverware, glasses, and plates, which were changed with each course.

It was also during the eighteenth century, in France, that restaurants as we think of them today came into existence (public eateries of a different sort existed as early as ancient Rome and China). A. Boulanger, a soup vendor, is widely credited as being the first restaurateur; he opened his business in Paris in 1765. The word *restaurant* is derived from the sign above the door to his establishment, which advertised "restaurants," meaning "restoratives" (from the French *restaurer*, to restore), referring to the soups and broths he offered. But it was the French Revolution (1789–1799) that launched the modern restaurant industry, producing most of the great chefs of history, who created many famous dishes. As French aristocrats fled the conflict in droves, they left behind their highly trained cooks, who began opening restaurants to serve the working class for the first time. By 1804, Paris had more than 500 restaurants.

More important during this period was the discovery of an effective method of preserving food. In 1795, General Napoleon Bonaparte offered a reward of 12,000 francs to the person who could find a way to keep food safe to eat for his troops, which were widely dispersed and, so, difficult to reach with supplies. Nicolas Appert

(1749–1841), a sometime brewer, confectioner, and chef, was the winner. He began experimenting with various techniques until, in 1809, he discovered that food could be successfully preserved if it were first heated to boiling and then sealed in airtight glass jars. Appert's method of boiling meat in a bain-marie prolonged the freshness of foods for several months, while also maintaining its quality. Napoleon proclaimed Appert "a benefactor to humankind."

Prior to Appert's revelation, food preservation techniques were rudimentary, primarily involving drying, salting, and smoking. Too often, however, foods preserved by these methods caused scurvy, in particular among sailors who were dependent on them on long voyages. Although Appert is known as the "father of canning," it wasn't until 1810 that the actual tin can was developed, by an Englishman, Peter Durand. He received a patent on the first tin-plated iron cylindrical canisters that, once sealed, were considered safe for the longer-term storage of food.

Another important development in the history of the buffet was menu composition. It was Georges Auguste Escoffier (1846–1935) who laid down the rules for the exact makeup and organization of a "menu." When planned properly from a gastronomical standpoint, a menu, he determined, should be in harmony with the mood of the host and his or her guests. The guests, in turn, must be inspired by the menu and almost able to express it. Escoffier also noted that the evolution of cuisine would constantly evolve, based on the changing tastes of the consumer. This concept was reiterated by Pellegrino Artusi (1820–1911), whose famous book *La scienza in cucina e l'arte di mangiore bene* (*Science in the Kitchen and the Art of Eating Well*) is considered a classic. Completed in 1891, it is still in print today, and Artusi is widely recognized as the creator of Italian cuisine.

The period between the end of the nineteenth century and World War I (1914–1918) was a wonderful one in the culinary arts, resulting in what is now known as "modern cuisine." After 1914, this evolution can be attributed to two essential factors: artificial refrigeration and a greater availability of funds. Both had a profound impact on all areas of the culinary arts.

MODERN BUFFETS

Buffets at the top hotels offered chefs an excellent arena in which to express their art. Items such as hams or whole fish covered in chaud-froid and decorated with truffles and aspic took center stage. Individual garnishes were created to decorate every platter. Fruits and vegetables were carved for presentation, as were desserts and elaborate sugar and chocolate work created by pastry chefs to draw attention to the table.

Buffets in the early days were thought of as an answer to the shortage of qualified staff at the front of the house. Not only did the buffet style of service eliminate the aggravation caused by untrained waitstaff, while meeting the challenge of providing formal service to the guest, a quality buffet also made it possible to present an appetizing display of food with great variety, allowed for more lead time for preparation, and became a showcase for the visual aspect of the culinary arts. And in its day, the all-you-can-eat-at-a-reasonable-price concept actually proved to be profitable. Imagine king crab legs, prawns, and beef tenderloin all featured on an all-you-can-eat buffet and priced less than a breakfast today would cost.

The challenge, however, was to ensure that the food on a buffet didn't just look good; it also had to be flavorful—it had to taste great. Sometimes, unfortunately, the art of food and its presentation took priority over how it tasted. Many items covered in sauces and topped with decoration were mysteries to the guest—what was underneath? Top chefs, in contrast, directed their focus to "edible food displays and art," as opposed to displays made with Styrofoam and other such materials. Ice carvings, pulled sugar, bread displays, and chocolate work were created to achieve the objective of visual beauty in food and food materials. Buffets were themed based on holidays, an event at hand, or interpretations of ethnic cuisines—which at the time were not as well understood as they are today.

As the cost of labor escalated, and the size of kitchens and their staffs diminished, the grand buffet became less and less grand. Even in the culinary show arena—dominated by large hotels that displayed over 20 feet of buffet with a variety of food for every taste, and works of art that looked too good to eat—they became less and less popular. Eventually, shows dropped the category altogether.

Buffets instead became a way to serve large volumes of people, with less attention paid to food quality than to quantity. People would flock to resorts and to early Las Vegas-type places for all-you-can-eat breakfast, lunch, and dinner buffets. Food at these venues was piled on steam tables, chafers, and counters to feed volumes and make money. Today, though a few of this type of buffet still exist, many more have given way to modern interpretations of the concept.

The one consistent fact about food is that it changes with the environment in which it is served. Las Vegas is a great example of this, where incredible hotels with signature restaurants and dining venues now dominate. People used to go to Las Vegas to gamble and see shows. Now they flock there to dine and shop.

Consequently, the Las Vegas buffets in the top hotels are more expensive today; they are also quality driven and presented in spaces designed to match their upscale image. They create an "experience" in the same way their signature restaurants do.

Nowadays, there also is a prevalent desire for authenticity, tradition, and "comfort cuisine." People are nostalgic, it seems, for the "great cuisines" of the past. But let us consider a cuisine that is "great" in a different way. This cuisine is diverse, has no boundaries, and is open to infinite creations; it is produced in an environment in which cooks and those who love good cooking can flourish.

The popularity of buffets continues, whether it is a simple, ceremonial, hot or cold buffet, or a buffet for an anniversary, cocktail party, breakfast, business luncheon, or political meeting. The expression of a cook's art is part of the ongoing buffet evolution, which features a festive dimension to food—whatever the occasion. Currently in the foodservice industry, there are more and more opportunities to hold a buffet service. This is because buffets are integral to many situations, from special occasions to no-frills business meetings. The celebration could be a personal or family occasion, such as a wedding, bar mitzvah, a special birthday (sweet-16 or centenarian) … the list goes on. In many hotels and clubs, the main stage for the buffet today is a holiday celebration, such as New Year's Eve, Christmas Eve, Mother's/Father's Day, or Thanksgiving.

Buffets also can be part of other types of social get-togethers, such as a clambake on the beach, a down-home barbeque, and many other themed events where dancing and socializing are the key attractions. At such events, the buffet allows people to intermingle with ease and talk with each other—often about the food on the buffet itself. Buffets at fundraisers or galas can be more elegant, such as the dine-around type (described in the next section).

Buffets are a common feature at many business meetings, conferences, and conventions, as they can offer an eat-while-you-work approach or a more simple form of service that does not take the time a three- or four-course served meal would. For large conventions, feeding 1,200 guests buffet style makes more sense than a sit-down breakfast, and can be more cost-effective as well.

Buffets are always planned event to event by the operation, often in conjunction with the host-client. The type and level of the buffet are driven by the objectives of the client, the event, and the available budget.

Visual decorations are important for buffet table presentations, to make a good impression on the guests. Old-style buffets featured decorations made out of ice, bread, vegetables, margarine, sugar, salt, and coated Styrofoam and were prepared a few days in advance. If well preserved, these materials could be used repeatedly.

In this book, you will find suggestions and instructions for decorations that use the food, the display, and other items, and that are simple to prepare yet are impressive. As for the food, especially cold food, you will learn about innovative techniques and modern equipment, like the combination oven ("combi oven"), the circulator, vacuum-sealing equipment, internal cooking thermometers, and flash freezers, all of which have changed the way we cook, display, and prepare our food.

Buffet Methodology

There are three areas you must take into consideration when planning a buffet:

- Types of Buffets
  - Selection of menu options
  - Dine-around buffet

- Working Techniques
  - Selection of foods
  - Preparation
  - Controlled cooking
  - Cooling

- The Display
  - Glazing
  - Garnishes
  - Decorations
  - Service vessels

Types of Buffets

Today, there is a wide variety of popular buffet types, ranging from reception buffets to lunch or dinner buffets to informal small buffets and dine-around buffets. In choosing the type of buffet for an event, it is very important to keep the following suggestions in mind:

- Choose ingredients that are in season, to bring freshness and a genuine character to the table. Keep in mind that fresh products are often more popular than imported or greenhouse products, and have the added advantage of costing less.

- During the winter, give preference to hot dishes; in the summer, serve cold dishes with plenty of vegetables.

- In preparing any type of buffet, aim to include meat, fish, cheese, vegetables, and starches that harmonize with the protein and fruit—in other words, offer something for everyone. When deciding on the proportions of these items, consider the client's needs and the type of event.

- Bear in mind the geographic location of the event, whether in or near the mountains, in a valley, or on a lake or by the ocean.

  - In mountainous regions, red meat is typically a first choice, along with more earthy type selections, followed by white meat and fish. Servings should always include lots of fruit, and some starches and vegetables that harmonize with the main proteins.

  - In a valley or flatland, give preference to white meat, followed by fish and red meat. Always serve sufficient quantities of vegetables and fruit.

  - When the event is located near a water body, give preference first to fish and other seafood, then to white or red meat. As always, provide an abundance of accoutrements.

  - To obtain a variety of flavors and tastes, cook the food in different ways, following solid cooking principles, such as roasting, sautéing, grilling, poaching, and braising. Be sure to accompany these items with the appropriate sauces, and use the proper cooking procedures. For example, a grilled selection might include a choice of salsas.

SELECTION OF MENU ITEMS

Base the selection of menu items for the buffet on the type of buffet that you want to prepare, as follows:

- A *reception buffet* is well suited for entertaining before lunch or dinner and is a pleasant way of welcoming guests. The menu should consist of finger foods, small sandwiches, modern shooters, fried foods, bite-size items on skewers, smoked fish, vegetables, salted pastries, and other small hot finger foods that are passed to the guests by waitstaff. When preparing trays of finger foods or traditional canapés and small sandwiches, use various types of breads: white bread, brioche, whole wheat, multigrain, and other flavored breads, such as a vanilla brioche for shellfish. Mix these breads with smoked and cured meats, fishes, salads, cheeses, and eggs, to provide something for everyone.

  Serve low-alcohol-content cocktails made with freshly squeezed fruit juices, dry sparkling wine, soft drinks, and soda water.

- *Luncheon or dinner buffets* may be served during meetings, conferences, and the like. In these cases, the buffet is typically made up of a few cold dishes or salads and one or two warm dishes—perhaps a soup, a first plate, a selection of main courses composed of meat, and one of fish served warm, with proper accoutrements and sauces. Other dishes should be composed of fresh seasonal vegetables and fruits that complement the main plates and give guests who do not eat meat or fish an alternative.

- *Informal buffets* are appropriate for short breaks of about half an hour, which always take place during conferences and meetings. During these pauses, it's appropriate to serve breakfast pastries and fruits, small canapés, small sandwiches, or a selection of pastries and cookies, as well as water, fruit juices, tea, and coffee. The menu will, of course, depend on the time of day the meeting or gathering is held.

DINE-AROUND BUFFET

Dine-around buffets are created for important celebrations, holidays, or events; as such, they require the most effort and energy from the kitchen and its entire staff, as compared to any other buffet. The entire organization and its team must work in harmony and in synchrony, both during the preparation phase and the actual service of the dine-around buffet.

Typically, the dine-around buffet incorporates elements of the old gala buffets, in concert with newest buffet trends and styles. For the dine-around buffet, the traditional single, very large buffet table displaying the majority of the menu is replaced with multiple stations. These stations are centered on a smaller main buffet table, and feature *action stations* as well as *stationary stations*. The goal is to spread out the traffic flow and offer tasting portions.

This type of buffet is becoming more and more popular, especially with catering and banquet services that are equipped to offer their professional services wherever they are needed. The dine-around buffet also allows the culinary team to express their artistic talents in full, while giving guests a new way to dine and enjoy buffet service.

ACTION STATIONS

If your buffet plans include action or demonstration stations, put the same thought into your menu for these stations as you would your à la carte menu. These buffet stations need to be more elaborate than the other buffet menu stations. Guests enjoy them because they see them as part of the dining experience; food is cooked, finished, or prepared in front of them. It's "showtime," when the menu item is sliced, tossed, plated, and presented to them as they watch and interact with the chef or cook. Thus, these stations offer the culinary team a chance to highlight their special talents, as they sauté meats or fish, finish a risotto, make bananas foster … the list goes on and on.

Similarly, a display of finger foods, artisanal cheeses, and meats benefit the guest when staffed by a knowledgeable attendant. The goodwill inherent in this approach ensures repeat customers and is a great public relations tool for your operation.

An action station may, however, add to the overall cost of the buffet, because you will have to dedicate at least one person to it, and this person must have the skills to execute the preparation of the food offered at station. In a self-promoted buffet, this becomes a labor cost, which means when selling to a client, you can add an attendant charge and get reimbursed for the labor being used.

On the other hand, one major advantage of an action station is food cost savings. Food is brought from the kitchen in its raw or a half-prepared state. The leftover food goes back to the kitchen, along with the backup food items in the kitchen. It can then be used for specials, another buffet, or for meals within the operation, keeping most of its value—as opposed to, say, three pans of prepared food that have sat in holding

boxes throughout the service. For a large event, the chef or cook can start cooking items and placing them on plates in a head service area, or prepare small batches, then place them in serving vessels to keep up with the volume.

Thanks to advances in equipment technology, such as the induction burner, griddles, turbo ovens, and more, the possibilities for the items that you can feature on an action station have expanded.

Action stations may even have more than one person working on a single item. For instance, an outside barbeque dine-around might feature three or more chefs in front of smokers, taking out the food then slicing brisket, cutting ribs, serving spoon bread, and more. These higher-end stations that require more staff are usually reserved for events where the cost can be passed on to the client, or for private clubs where membership has its benefits.

An action station or two can be featured at a social reception that features passed hors d'oeuvres and stationary food displays and that also has a chef cooking or preparing small plates, which are passed to the guest, or carving a protein food item. At sushi stations chefs may make sushi in front of the guests, to add to the experience.

In practice, these stations borrow a page from the modern open-restaurant kitchens where guests can see all the action. The action station takes this one step further, by encouraging interaction between guests and staff, freedom of choice, and a more social way to dine. At large events, the buffet usually includes traditional buffet tables for salads, first-plate-type items, and then is surrounded by buffet action stations that ease the traffic flow while producing a completely new, modern buffet experience.

Finally, these stations require embellishments—culinary decorations that are works of art in and of themselves. They are made of edible materials such as butter or margarine, bread, sugar, chocolate, sculptured fruit and vegetables, ice, and more, to create a display that is pleasant to the eye and stimulating to the appetite. There may also be decorations or props that are appropriate to the event or holiday, in the form of flowers, statues, or ceramic figures that complement the stations.

Working Techniques

When preparing buffets, specific techniques are required to ensure that food is prepared properly and in hygienic conditions, to avoid foodborne illnesses. Close attention must be paid to preparing food according to standards, to avoid contamination—any cook's worst enemy, especially because most buffet dishes need advance preparation and are served and displayed in a variety of venues and temperatures.

FOOD SELECTION

Buy food that is absolutely fresh and pleasant looking, and transport it to the kitchen in proper, refrigerated containers. Once delivered, remove the food from the containers in which it was transported and place it in new ones to be stored in suitable refrigeration. Clean fruit and vegetables of any dirt and wilted parts and check for signs of deterioration; then place produce in containers that allow proper airflow.

Place meats, game, and poultry—anything derived from animals—in suitable closed containers, and, if possible, in separate refrigeration to prevent cross-contamination. It is advisable to vacuum-pack cured fish

and meat in order to ensure the freshness of the product. Ideally, store these dishes in separate storage containers.

Fish and seafood need their own refrigeration at, ideally, 37°F (3°C), and should be iced when possible.

FOOD PREPARATION

Since the food should be prepared and consumed quickly, all rules of hygiene must be observed. Hands and uniforms should be clean and well kept; hair should be pulled back and covered. When chefs or cooks go out to work buffet stations, they should put on a fresh jacket, not wear the one they worked in all day.

Food preparation should take place in clean kitchens with counters that have been sanitized beforehand. Ideally, temperatures in this controlled environment will remain constant: The raw food product should not rise above 38°F (3°C). All cooking, serving, and display equipment and tools should be checked thoroughly.

Initial preparation begins with the cutting of meats, fish, vegetables, and garnish items. From there, move on to any planned blanching, searing, grilling, and the making of terrines, jellies, pâtés, mousses, salads, and casserole dishes. The final steps are the cooking, holding, and plating.

CONTROLLED COOKING

It hardly need be said that cooking is a critical aspect in the buffet preparation process. Using gauges or thermometers to check food, you can visually and accurately track the various phases of the cooking process, to ensure proper and safe cooking, and, more importantly, monitor food during the holding process. In batch cooking, controlled temperatures mean that fewer liquids will be lost and food will maintain a higher nutritional value. Food also will retain its shape and firmness when presented or sliced and, thus, be more appealing to the guest. Furthermore, temperature gauges eliminate the need to make calculations based on weight, oven temperature, or the amount of water. Modern kitchen equipment includes gauges that have an automatic shutoff feature that engages when the desired temperature is reached, and combi ovens that use dry heat with steam to keep moisture in the product.

From roasting, braising, poaching, or cooking sous vide, the possibilities for producing flavorful, healthy, and safe food for buffets keep this style of food service popular with guests. Keep in mind, however, as noted previously, that the dine-around buffet does require the finishing or cooking of some products in front of the guest, so extra precautions must be taken to ensure that food stays safe.

COOLING

Once a dish is cooked, its temperature must be lowered and the dish cooled as quickly as possible. Food can be immersed in water, ice, or salt (with or without wrappings) to hasten the cooling process.

Cooling is also possible now using new equipment such as flash freezers, which are made especially to chill solid and liquid substances quickly. This prevents bacteria from developing and ensures a longer life for the dish. When placed in a high vacuum or treated with inert gas, the life of the dish increases even more.

Some examples of modern refrigeration that assist in the rapid cooling are shown here.

A blast chiller takes hot food to a safe, cold temperature in a short amount of time.

The Display

Buffets, plain and simple, are visual displays that should entice the guest to partake of its offerings. Whether the buffet is a continental breakfast or working lunch, the standards followed and effort given to create it should be consistent and of high quality. Four important items play a role in the success of your buffet display:

1. Glazing or preservation of the food
2. Garnishing
3. Decoration
4. Selection of service vessels

When these four items are handled correctly and come together, the display of your buffet will be one that pleases the guest and speaks volumes about the quality of your operation.

GLAZING

The original purpose of glazing was to protect sliced food on platters from oxidation and airborne bacteria. Although some guests do not care for gelatin, it has historically been used in buffets. There are new techniques to greatly reduce the thickness of the gelatin so that it is lighter and more appealing to even the most discriminating palates. Making gelatin from reduced stocks that reflect the product being glazed also adds much to the flavor profile of the dish or product. There is no doubt that glazing lends splendor to dishes and enhances their colors.

Though modern-style buffets no longer include large presentations of sliced meats and fish on silver platters, glazing or preservation of the food remains essential to preserving its appearance and fresh look. For finger foods, small plates, and sliced items, a light coat of gelatin or glazing, made using more modern techniques, should become a standard practice for your high-quality buffet.

After slicing meat, fish, or vegetable terrines, arrange slices on stainless-steel or plastic platters and brush lightly with gelatin, to coat. Or use flavored oils, dressings, light sauces, spices, flavored powders, and a variety of salts, herbs, and pepper as alternatives for coating displayed food so it does not dry out. Doing so also will infuse flavor to the food. Even when presenting a tossed salad, the greens tossed very lightly with an extra-virgin olive oil will have a nice sheen, add to the flavor profile of the dressing the guest chooses, and present well.

Assembling a well-balanced platter or plate of food is important, to ensure that it is neither too full nor too heavy. Arrange the main food product artistically; a good rule of thumb is to make side dishes and garnishes proportional to the volume and weight of the main items. Serve sauces in separate vessels, and be sure to include enough of each sauce for every portion of food.

Large platters have given way to smaller platters or large plates and other types of serviceware that are unique to modern buffets. The thought process behind the new methodology of buffet service is to make it easier to replenish the line with fresher food, so that the buffet always looks consistently appealing and plentiful throughout the service.

GARNISHES

Garnishing food is another essential aspect of the buffet process, as the food and its presentation, together, make the buffet come alive. The art of garnishing food, though, has changed greatly over time. Tomato roses, bunches of herbs, and covering food with sauces have made way for a more natural approach. Smaller plates of food arranged in an elegant manner, along with garnishes

This is a striking example of an ice carving used as a functional decoration for service. In this case, sushi and shellfish are displayed on the ice carving. Not only is it a functional service centerpiece, but it keeps the seafood items at a safe serving temperature.

of cut and marinated vegetables, fried herb leaves, or crispy elements, make for garnishes that offer flavor, are part of the dish, and are edible.

Here is a 12-point program for garnishing your buffet food:

1. Hot food, hot garnish.

2. Cold food, cold garnish.

3. Make garnishes edible.

4. Avoid overgarnishing; the garnish is meant to complement, not dominate, the food.

5. Take care that the flavors of the garnish complement the food it garnishes; diced salami over lobster salad is not a good idea, for example.

6. Do not overcrowd your plate or platter with garnish; doing so reduces the appeal of the food.

7. Use knife-cutting skills and a variety of knife cuts to create a natural but effective garnish.

8. Always plan the garnish and its amount so the guest can recognize the main item.

9. Work with flavor garnishes such as spiced oils, syrups, dried fruits, and powders to add visual attraction and incorporate flavor.

10. Garnish with texture; for example, fried basil over mozzarella and tomato adds flavor, as well as contrast and texture to a salad, as opposed to chopped fresh basil.

11. Garnish using the yin-and-yang concept; for example, a plate of smoked salty duck breast with a sweet garnish of fruit quenelles works well.

12. Always garnish with simplicity and elegance as your goals.

DECORATIONS

Decorations are, of course, crucial to the overall look and presentation of a buffet. That said, and though they still play a major role in buffet presentation, the days of large sculptures, tallow, sprayed Styrofoam™, and ice are not as common in modern buffets, due to cost, the lost art of the craft, and the new style that favors more sleek and elegant presentations.

Nevertheless, some of these more traditional decoration items still can be used to good effect on the buffet table. A milkshake bar (page 156) uses ice sculpture as a functional centerpiece: It holds the milkshakes glasses for the customer and adds a wow factor, making the ice piece practical as well as part of the theme. Another example is an ice shrimp bowl that holds poached shrimp, with parsley and lemons, as garnish, making for a striking presentation that, again, is functional as well as decorative.

Other materials such as flowers, ferns, lemon leaves, and props can be used to decorate the stations. A station serving Italian food might, for example, be accented with glass bottles of olive oil and vinegar and a basket of assorted dry pastas, to capture the theme and concept of the station.

Classic buffets that used skirted tables as a decoration, to add color and dimension, have given way to fitted skirts and finished tabletops with no linens. Another clean and elegant way to decorate is to use antique tables in place of linen and skirted tables.

Following is a 10-point decoration program for buffets:

1. Choose decorations that complement the buffet or buffet station; they should not detract from the food being featured or get in the way of service.

2. Incorporate props that embrace the theme of the buffet or station; but keep them to a minimum.

3. Decorate back tables at action stations so as to detract from the utensils or unprepared food on the table.

4. Choose decorations that give the impression of action; stay away from anything that makes the buffet seem static. Another way to accomplish this is by utilizing different heights, shapes, and colors.

5. Enlist a person on staff who has artistic ability and a sense of style to create the decorations.

6. When using fruit or vegetables as decoration, make sure the products are of the freshest nature and color; remove any stickers of origin, wipe them clean, and arrange them in an artistic manner that balances height and style.

7. Don't forget proper lighting: LCD lights and colored lighting can enhance the buffet table and station. Lights that accentuate the centerpiece or chocolate work on a pastry buffet make it all the more memorable.

8. Incorporate staff uniforms in decorations. Cooks and chefs wearing a modern chef's coat, perhaps accented by black or gold buttons, a striped apron, and European cap, create a striking addition to the overall presentation.

9. Use backdrops for buffet stations positioned against a wall; these make for excellent decorations while keeping table space available for food and service.

10. As with the food, remember that simplicity combined with elegance results in the greatest achievement.

SERVICE VESSELS

In the past, buffet designers used a silver tray (better known as "the platter") as the canvas for presenting buffet food. Mirrors were used, as well, but silver dominated. In the late 1990s, chefs who managed buffets, and their competitors, began to look for other options.

Without question, silver trays still make for a stunning foundation, but they present challenges, as well:

- Quality silver trays are expensive.

- They require a great deal of care and upkeep. Regular polishing, along with resurfacing of the silver, is needed after long-term use, due to scratches from normal wear and tear.

- When used for food presentation, a layer of gelatin, called a glaze, has to be poured over the platter. This is an art in itself.

- Silver trays are limited in the sizes and shapes available.

More modern buffet styles and dine-arounds still use the classic look of silver trays for food display. However, alternatives such as marble, acrylic, and polished stone have all come of age, allowing the chef greater flexibility, as service vessels made of these materials can be designed and cut to specific sizes and shapes.

As buffets continue to evolve, large trays are, in general, becoming outdated. The objective is to display smaller quantities of food and replenish more often so that the food on the buffet or buffet station is fresh, and every guest, regardless of when he or she arrives at the buffet, receives the same level of quality as the first guest.

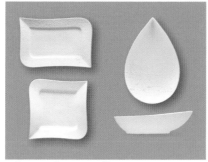

Source: Courtesy of Fortessa, Inc.

This small assortment of china plates make it easy to implement the simple-but-elegant approach in your food displays. The china is white, which is a great backdrop to showcase the food. The surface area is large, but not too large, and leaves room to display the food with elegance.

China and glassware have become the dominant display vessels on buffet tables today. China development has progressed the most over the past 10 years, in design, styling, and the variety of shapes and materials used. A china platter or plate of about 13 to 15 inches makes an excellent canvas for food. It allows you to institute a system of replenishment that keeps the buffet looking as it should, from the time it opens until the time it closes.

Here are a number of helpful guidelines to follow when planning your buffet service vessel program:

1. Keep buffet china, service vessels, and utensils separate from à la carte service items.

2. Attach a Polaroid photo or digital picture printout on storage shelves to indicate what goes where.

3. Keep a standards manual on hand that shows each salad or food item and the plate on which it should be displayed. Train staff using visuals, to ensure consistency.

4. Involve your steward team in the care and storage of all buffet serviceware, trays, heat lamps, tables, and other items. Remember, they are the gatekeepers of all equipment, so seek their input on the best ways to store and handle your investment in buffet items.

5. Store bowls and other specialty items that are used for condiments and sauces in an area marked accordingly, for both the front and back of the house.

6. When storing items made of glass and other fragile materials, insert felt other soft liners between each, and limit their number in a stack, to prevent breakage.

7. For larger items such as grill tops, chafers, and heat lamps, invest in storage boxes; they will pay for themselves.

8. Place small specialty plates for tastings and other small plates first in bus buckets and then in a metro shelving cart on wheels with locking doors.

9. When glass is in service, be aware that very hot or very cold temperatures will promote breakage, which then adds up to the loss of the plate plus the food displayed on it.

10. Do not buy china or service vessels for looks alone; before purchasing, also take into account practicality, durability, and user-friendliness.

11. Think twice before choosing colored china; food always displays best on white or neutral colors, which also blend well regardless of the buffet tabletop colors or themes.

12. Fresh is in, so stockpile enough china or service vessels so that you can replenish your largest possible buffet function in a timely manner.

Simple Blueprint for Successful Planning

Most buffets are sold through sales and catering departments. The client and the particular theme are the starting points for developing your plan for the buffet itself. The success of a buffet requires that the food and its presentation complement—not overshadow—the event or occasion. This is a fine balance to achieve.

A holiday buffet, such as one for Easter, would center around the holiday, from the décor to the food—perhaps featuring lamb on the menu. The meal period is a big factor in the planning, as well. A brunch would feature omelets and some breakfast fare, whereas a dinner buffet might include salads and a selection of cold items, along with hot main plate selections presented in tasting portions.

The time of year, the weather, and, of course, the guests' comfort and expectations are also factors in how you create and maintain the theme of your buffet. Your blueprint or plan will take all these factors into account, as together and separately they will influence and direct the specific dishes and menu for the buffet, as well as the overall presentation, from decoration to presentation of the food.

Each stage of your buffet blueprint—the setup, decorations, menu plan, staff assignments, replenishment, and maintenance of the buffet during the event—works in harmony with the others to ensure the buffet is a success.

A *featured-concept buffet* is one that hotels and private clubs have been promoting for years. Sunday brunch buffets, all-you-can-eat seafood buffets, and the increasingly popular "quick service" breakfast or lunch menus (common in hotel chains or restaurants with limited resources) can work well for both the customer and the operator. An excellent example can be found at the Waldorf–Astoria in New York City. It is well known for its Sunday brunch, served in the Peacock Room, which offers every type of cuisine, made-to-order eggs Benedict, a seafood bar, and a pastry display that is simply amazing.

In a featured-concept buffet, the chef selects menu items that have customer appeal and also help to improve the operation's bottom line by utilizing foods from other kitchens or banquet events. The most popular featured-concept buffet is the breakfast buffet. Operations that regularly serve some form of breakfast buffet include hotels, resorts, private clubs, country clubs, casinos, and the new-style courtyard and inn hotels that do not have full-service restaurants.

The smaller version of a breakfast buffet, called the *continental*, serves items such as muffins, croissants, and Danish pastries, fresh fruit, bagels, and accoutrements; coffee, tea, juices, and milk; and a selection of yogurts and cereal. In Europe and at the new-style hotels, guests receive a "value-added" experience by having breakfast included in the room rate.

The menu from a more extensive breakfast buffet might include an omelet station and many individual breakfast items, such as scrambled eggs, bacon, waffles, hash browns, quiche, and the previously mentioned foods served in resorts and convention and conference venues.

Keys to Creating a Successful Buffet Blueprint

The blueprint guidelines offered here are for those operations that must feed large numbers quickly and efficiently. However, no matter what the buffet concept of the operation, a blueprint and plan will ensure consistency, and that its goals and objectives are achieved, from both the operator's standpoint and, most importantly, that of its guests!

MENU DEVELOPMENT

This section describes the process of developing a menu that will both meet the guest's or client's goals and turn a profit for the restaurant. It is the responsibility of the entire team, from the sales and catering staff to the culinary staff, to develop a buffet menu that conforms to the theme, meets the objectives of the client, and adheres to the budget of both the client and the property.

You can create a unique dining experience by ensuring that the menu selections and the presentation

of your food, along with the buffet décor, convey a message of quality to the guest. Remember, buffet-style service offers guests variety, the freedom to choose what they like to eat, and how much (portion size), and the opportunity to experience many types of food.

Keys to Menu Development

- Establish the appropriate menu selections for the buffet based on the client's desires, needs, and budget.

- Identify the number of options within each of the selected categories.

- Draft a potential menu, taking into account any special requests, in conjunction with the theme or purpose of the buffet.

- Keep in mind that guests expect to see variety in all selections on a buffet menu, from salads to desserts.

- Select menu items from previous events that have been successful and have gained customer appeal. The advantage to this is that you already know the standards, from the presentation and décor to the food recipes.

- Offer new items that reflect popular trends in both eating habits and diets and that enable you to try out new concepts or designs.

- Keep in mind that buffets can also serve as a creative and profitable outlet for a wide variety of foods, when you utilize items in-house and price your buffets properly.

- Be sure that the menu is one that meets customers' expectations and, at the same time,

showcases the facilities and the skills of both the front- and back-of-house staff.

- Always remember the décor; the room setup and food presentation create an expectation of excitement for the experience for the guest.

- Ensure that your staff can execute the menu items to meet the expectations of the guests and client.

MANAGING BUFFET COSTS

As you begin to develop your menu, you need to establish the price points for your buffet. There are a number of factors to consider; in particular, in a commercial setting, the competition's price may come into play. The pricing you decide on also will determine the number of options you can offer on the buffet, as well as the specific ingredients that you include on the menu. A pasta station, for example, will have a lower price point than a station carving rack of lamb.

Menu mix, as in à la carte service, also plays a role in cost management. A lunch buffet serving a crab salad can be offset by featuring other attractive but less costly salads to balance out your food cost.

Food costs for in-house buffets can be problematic to estimate because it is difficult to predict the exact number of guests. Even for client-driven buffet events, which have a set number of guests, there is no way of knowing whether guests will eat the foods you prepared in the amounts and/or portions you prepared.

To help address these factors as accurately as possible, it's critical to first gain a clear understanding of the event and the guests who will attend. At large elegant buffets, a wide selection of food options also means smaller portions, and the chef should approach the buffet as a tasting menu. In contrast, a buffet that will serve all-male guests from the construction industry will need to feature a heavy portion of grilled steak and other items that hungry men would enjoy.

In addition to the cost of the food for a buffet, labor costs also must be monitored and managed. To accomplish this, ask questions such as: What should the ratio of chef-to-guest be for action stations? How many runners per number of guests will be needed to ensure that the buffet looks fresh at all times? (Note that for client events, you may be able to charge a fee for station chefs and/or attendants.)

Equipment cost is another important factor in assuring profitability for an operation. It's essential that your steward team be trained to maintain proper standards of care for your equipment. (Review the section on service vessels for tips on how to manage your investment.)

Top 10 Tips for Controlling Buffet Costs

1. Batch cook and batch mix buffet dishes as needed. Foods must be at the height of quality when presented. Many buffet foods are prepared well in advance and then held in heating cabinets; similarly, salads are mixed with dressings and set to serve. This does not give the impression of quality and freshness to the guest, and produces leftovers that can cause food cost issues.

2. Review each menu item to determine if it imposes any restrictions with regard to food cost, the pace of service to fill and refill the items, the overall budget, the equipment needed, and the talent/skill of the buffet attendants.

3. Keep in mind that carved meats and other buffet stations lend themselves well to buffet service. Review other menu items that must be prepared à la minute and served immediately or are fragile in nature, such as foie gras.

This type of item may require special handling during its preparation and for the presentation; thus, it may not be cost-effective.

4. Remember that not all dishes are equally suitable for buffets. Serving rare duck for a buffet of 200 may be a challenge; a better idea is to present such a dish at an action station. Foods such as pasta, omelets, scaloppini, and risotto that are made or finished to order impress guests, are fresh when served, and produce no leftover waste because the ingredients can be reused from a fresh state, giving you full food cost value.

5. Include a surcharge in your buffet blueprint for chefs or other attendants to offset labor costs. And give the guest a choice between self-serve food or more personalized service and a fresher product.

6. Get every dollar of buffet sales. Charge for beverages, soft drinks, after-dinner coffee and tea; or include beverages in the final buffet pricing.

7. Try to up-sell the client. A milkshake bar, pastry display, or sushi station can demand a premium, giving the operation a chance to impress its guests. For you, extra profit as labor is already accounted for, and low food cost items for buffets can make money; their presentation and wow factor are what sells.

8. Use a ratio of 1 chef per every 100 guests for a buffet action station spread over 2 hours or more. Staff 2 runners for every 100 guests, to keep the buffet refilled and fresh.

9. Manage your operational expenses. Linens, paper, decorations, and a florist add to operational costs, affect the bottom line, and need just as much attention as food and labor costs.

10. Leave no detail to chance. Take advantage of every opportunity to meet and exceed customers' expectations while creating a balance between cost control and freedom of choice for the guest.

PLANNING THE BUFFET

Research and planning are the keys to a successful buffet. Once you have the blueprint, menu, standards, and systems in place, the buffet process is easy. Then, you can make raising the bar and establishing new benchmarks in buffet service your new goals.

Follow these guidelines and you will be on your way to offering exceptional and elegant buffet service, regardless of the occasion.

Blueprint Guidelines for Planning Your Buffet

- Make a drawing and plan of the buffet area for the event. This includes a template of the room, the tables needed for the buffet, and where they will go. You may want to make your blueprint more detailed and include which items go where on the buffet stations and the buffet table.

- Have standard blueprints for each function room and its layout; this will assist in creating a more detailed blueprint.

- Make sure the blueprint includes a plan to help you meet all of your buffet objectives: great food, outstanding service, a memorable experience that exceeds your customer's expectations, and, at the end of the day, fiscal results that achieve your operation's financial objectives.

- Ensure that your buffet provides maximum service with the minimum labor cost by instituting a ratio

of staff per guest at a higher level than for à la carte service.

- To safeguard the freshness of the product for the event, organize food production and establish batch food practices to control waste.

- The quality of your buffet speaks volumes about the reputation of your operation, so no matter how small the buffet service or type of event, follow the standards you set in your blueprint.

- Review your plan or blueprint with all staff members who will be assisting in the preparation and service of your buffet, so that everyone is on the same page.

- Post a time schedule and area of responsibility for each team member.

- Ideally, use separate tables for pastry and beverage service.

- Always keep in mind that, from the guest's point of view, the three main advantages of buffets are speed of service, variety of choices, and amount of food offered.

- More is not always better—follow this rule of thumb: smaller plates and platters refreshed more often.

- Keep all decoration items in boxes and containers marked with an inventory of what each box holds and for which events they are used.

- Never let the buffet stations or buffet tables give the impression of being static; use different levels of height along with various shapes, materials, and textures to give the buffet an action feel.

- Do not invest a lot of time in creating or planning displays and items that cannot be eaten or do not serve a purpose in the service of the food.

- Aim for authenticity in both food and décor; this is the key to the success of themed buffets. Study the pantry of a country or region carefully, review current cuisine trends, and ensure that the menu contains food that presents and holds well for buffet service.

- Follow the rule of simplicity and elegance in everything you do.

- Remember, the larger the buffet, the more traffic planning you'll have to do. Stations and buffet food items, when properly planned for and located, can ensure traffic moves smoothly and efficiently.

- Take into account when menu planning—and especially for staffing—that larger events may need double buffet stations to serve the guest properly. If you set up 4 action stations for a buffet of 500 people, then you'll need 8 cooks to staff the stations.

Buffets have stood the test of time. They are adaptable and versatile to all kinds of foodservice venues and service styles, as well as many customer price points. The key to a successful buffet is in the planning.

From five-star hotels to simple chains, buffets are part of the dining experience all over the world. In the coming chapters you'll read about buffets that will inspire you, and about menu items that will drive your passion to create, to think outside the box. Chapter 2 starts by describing buffets for the most important meal of the day: breakfast. The breakfast buffet, more than any other type, is popular globally and is regarded as the most customer-friendly style of service.

Dinner Buffet

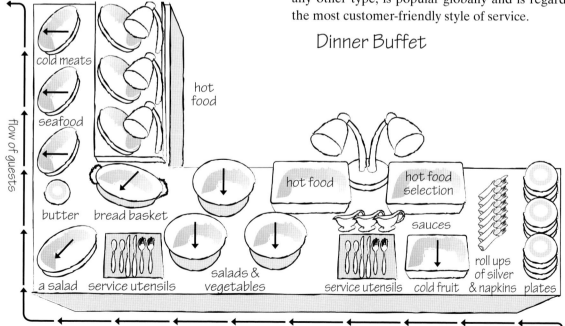

Blueprint for a dinner buffet.

CHAPTER TWO

SENSATIONAL BREAKFASTS

It is said that the most important way to start your day is with a good breakfast. No wonder, then, that the breakfast buffet has become a staple of many hotels, clubs, and resorts. The usual fare of eggs, bacon, sausage, and morning pastries has been featured on countless buffets. Many hotels offer breakfast buffets as a value-add to help sell rooms and as a way to offer a complete package. In Europe, rooms typically are sold with the option to include breakfast—sometimes referred to as the "American plan." The continental breakfast is a traditional concept, one that is still popular today. Offering an array of baked goods, cereal, and fresh fruit, along with a guest's morning beverage selections, this self-service approach saves on labor costs for the hotel and time for the guest. Many hotel concepts offer a self-service breakfast buffet with continental dishes as its foundation. Added to the foundation

are eggs, bacon, sausage, and potatoes, in chafers. Sometimes, pancakes or make-your-own waffles and other selections are offered.

This type of buffet lets guests choose what they would like to eat, and take as much as they want, while saving time and labor for the operator, making it possible to serve a large customer base with almost less than one-quarter the labor of an à la carte service. Upscale dining operations and the finer hotels will have chefs cooking at action stations, making omelets to order, waffles, and other breakfast treats. Such buffets are of a high standard, but also increase the price of breakfast immensely.

Display of cereal, fruit, and fruit shooters with coffee cake on continental breakfast buffet.

Breakfast meetings and morning events rely heavily on the breakfast buffet style of service. But this meal has often presented a quandary for most operators: It is a challenge to take menu fare that is a staple for so many and evolve it into something elegant and that meets the standard of other meal periods. It has also a challenge to motivate the staff for this service, especially the culinary team. Breakfast cookery, as compared to lunch, and even more so dinner, is regarded as the least desirable of the three.

Menu for Continental Breakfast

BAGELS, VARIETY OF MUFFINS

Braided coffee cake, cinnamon chocolate coffee cake, assorted Danish pastries

Freshly sliced seasonal fruit, fruit shooters, and yogurt parfaits

Fresh fruit in pineapple boats with yogurt and berries

Juices, cereal, croissants

THE DETAILS

Butter, cream cheese, jams, jellies

BUFFET DETAILS

Toaster, plates, roll-up utensils, glasses, serving spoons, risers, small plates

gets to the hotel at 6:00 AM. Knowing the hours required to oversee such a large hotel—which maintains more than eight dining venues, hosts banquets, and promotes dinner concepts of the highest level—one would think a chef of his caliber would focus on lunch, important banquets, and the dinner hour. But, he explained, the hotel runs at 90 percent occupancy, and the majority of the guests are out for the day on business or sightseeing. So while the hotel does capture a percentage of its guests for dinner, the breakfast service experiences the highest level of their participation with regard to hotel dining. Thus, for Chef Otto, breakfast is the most important meal at the hotel. Three venues are open at the hotel for breakfast, and they serve the majority of the hotel guests; for them, that dining experience is their introduction to the quality of food the hotel provides. Therefore, Chef Otto and his staff take as much pride in developing menus and food standards—and modern presentations—for breakfast as they do for dinner.

Furthermore, the perception of some of a breakfast cook or chef may not be as high as that of the dinner chef, who is seen as a craftsperson capable of cooking the finest of fare. The motivation, though, should be clear and simple: A high standard of quality must be consistent across all meal periods and all foods, from breakfast to dinner and from an omelet to a hamburger to a filet mignon.

I remember a conversation I had with Chef Otto Weibal of the Fairmont Hotel in Singapore. At dinner one night we were discussing cuisine, food trends, and new meal concepts, along with our job responsibilities. I was surprised to learn that a few days each week he

Furthermore, if Chef Otto, as the lead person on the food and beverage team, did not show up during breakfast to work, inspect, and train, what message would he be sending to the culinary staff? No doubt they would wonder: If the chef is never on site for the first meal of the day, how important is what we do? How important is breakfast to the hotel and guests? That is why Chef Otto's executive sous chef and the entire team of sous chefs all take responsibility for breakfast; they work on a revolving schedule to ensure their presence at the restaurants serving breakfast and at banquet functions that are breakfast oriented.

I gained new insight and understanding from Chef Otto that evening: that any meal, no matter how simple, no matter the fare, should be held to the same high standard as a VIP banquet, wine dinner, or award-winning dinner restaurant.

With that lesson in mind, I set off to reinvent my approach to breakfast service. I was determined to think outside the box—not just in terms of how food is displayed but also in terms of how to develop new and innovative breakfast items, but derived from tried-and-true breakfast classics, so that guests would have a comfort level with them. For no matter how creative culinarians or management may like to be, or how exciting a concept or menu is, the proof of success lies with the end user—the guest must accept it.

Breakfast Buffet (small)* for 50 to 60

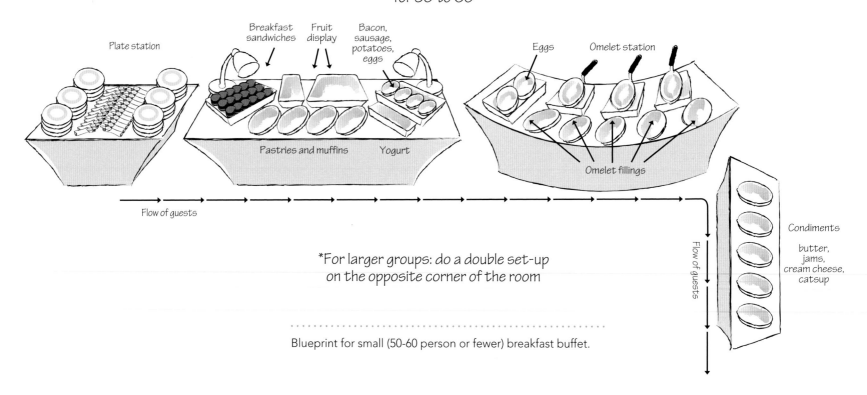

*For larger groups: do a double set-up on the opposite corner of the room

Blueprint for small (50-60 person or fewer) breakfast buffet.

This calls to mind a quote from Marie-Antoine Carême (1784–1833), "the king of chefs and the chef of kings," which remains true today: "In the matters of cookery, there are not a number of principles, there is only one; and that is to satisfy the person you are serving." This is even more evident today, when guests are much more knowledgeable, demand value for their money, and want that trust factor where they dine. I have found that trying something new but basing it on something old is very fruitful—not only from the creativity standpoint but also, and more importantly, from the standpoint of guest acceptance.

Take, for example, a version of eggs Benedict (page 31). The concept is based one of the most popular menu items there is. Whether it is offered for breakfast, brunch, à la carte service, or buffet service, eggs Benedict is a winner. The development process I use for new buffet menu items is simple: It is called a *deconstruction process*. In this case, I take all the main components of traditional eggs Benedict and then interchange them to create a variety of new menu ideas. Doing this also builds trust with guests and encourages them to try new flavor concepts. They know what eggs Benedict are and enjoy it because they are comfortable with it. This, then, makes it more likely that they will try different versions of this longtime favorite, especially when it is made with items such as short ribs or lobster, other customer favorites.

The following pages introduce three breakfast concepts based on traditional fare that respects the foundation of the original dish yet lends a touch of creativity. You will see how easy it is to develop great buffet cuisine while adhering to what I consider to be the most important rule, which I repeat throughout the book: *Simplicity with elegance.* This is the key. Simplicity in service and preparation. Simplicity for the end user, your guest. By following this rule, guests can more readily relate to, understand, and be enticed by your food. Not only do elegant presentations of food, flavorful menus, and the buffet setup showcase the talents of the property, they give your guests a great dining experience, one with a "wow factor."

Refer to Chapters 12 and 13, as well, which present a few stations that place breakfast on the same par as any other food station on the buffet line.

BREAKFAST SPRING ROLLS

Spring rolls are a favorite of Asian cuisines and others around the world. There are, as with most types of food, a wide variety of spring rolls. For our breakfast spring rolls, we take the Thai approach, using rice paper to produce a healthy but flavorful alternative to breakfast fare. The beauty of this concept is threefold:

- Spring rolls are a recognized item with customer appeal.

- The style of the spring roll used here works well as a healthy alternative and vegetarian choice for the buffet diner today who seeks this type of offering. He or she will be pleasantly surprised to see food such as this on a buffet.

- It is creative at the same time it is simplistic in nature and full of flavor; and the variety of fillings is endless, and showcases freshness and flavor.

Chef Leonard's Breakfast Spring Rolls | SERVES 6 TO 12

INGREDIENTS

Dipping Sauce

1 tsp / 5 ml	Crushed red pepper flakes
1/3 cup / 80 ml	Rice wine vinegar
2/3 cup / 160 ml	Mushroom soy sauce
1 tsp / 5 ml	Brown sugar
2 tbsp / 30 ml	Lime juice, freshly squeezed
1 tsp / 5 ml	Minced garlic
1/3 cup / 80 ml	Pineapple juice

Spring Rolls

1 cup / 225 g	Carrots, peeled and cut julienne
1 cup / 225 g	Bean sprouts
2	Scallions, cut into slivers
1 tbsp / 30 g	Basil leaves, roughly chopped
6	Eggs, scrambled soft (warm)
6 slices	Bacon, cooked and diced (warm)
1/2 cup / 115 g	Cheddar cheese, grated
1/3 cup / 80 ml	Plum sauce
6 sheets	Rice paper,* 8–10 in. (20–25 cm) in diameter

These spring rolls are a twist from savory Vietnamese-style spring rolls. They offer a nice alternative for the guest, are healthy, and can be baconless to meet vegetarian choices.

For rice paper, have a bowl larger than the diameter of the spring roll sheets so that you can completely immerse the paper in water to soak and soften.

Method

1. Whisk together all of the dipping sauce ingredients and set aside.

2. To prepare the spring rolls, in a bowl, mix the carrots, bean sprouts, scallions, and basil with 2 tsp (10 ml) of the dipping sauce.

3. Set out a bowl of warm water and a clean kitchen towel; line up the eggs, bacon, and cheese, along with the carrot mix and plum sauce, across the towel.

4. Fully immerse a sheet of rice paper into the water for about 15 to 20 seconds. Lay it on the towel.

5. Spread a teaspoon of the plum sauce in the middle of the rice paper.

6. Leaving a half inch on each side of the paper, add some of the carrot mix first, then some of the cheese and bacon, and, finally, the egg.

7. Fold and roll up the rice paper, keeping it fairly tight. Place the finished rolls in a serving vessel.

8. Serve with dipping sauce.

OMELET STATION

Omelets are a longtime customer favorite. Opportunities for creativity in their preparation are, however, limited, as the foundation of the station is eggs, with a variety of fillings from which the guest can choose. The presentation and setup of the station are key to ensuring your omelet station has synergy with the other offerings on your buffet. Fresh ingredients can be showcased in modern-design vessels, alongside a variety of other items, such as breakfast or brunch pastry.

Another option is to upscale your omelet station—if the price point and event allows it. For holiday brunch buffets or dine-arounds, we have done this with great success. Items such as baby shrimp, jumbo lump crab, asparagus cuts, olive oil tomatoes, smoked salmon, and sliced tenderloin for a steak-and-egg omelet have proven popular and taken the typical omelet station to new heights.

Even the basic omelet station executed with care can exemplify quality and satisfy the customer that your operation is of the highest standard. In some ways, it is at the simplest stations where you can most easily exceed customers' expectations. For example, the majority of people do not look to an omelet station for something special; thus, when you give them something that grabs their attention, they are very impressed.

There is, as with any cooking procedure, a right way and a wrong way to make an omelet. A good omelet should be light, not dry, and the ratio of ingredients not overwhelming to the egg. Your ingredients should be cut properly, to showcase them. Ham diced correctly and consistently looks skillful and enticing, as opposed to being chopped haphazardly or sloppily, which conveys a different image. Blanching vegetables or par sautéing them not only saves time with made-to-order omelet preparation, but makes them look more appetizing. Picture caramelized onions, roasted mushrooms, and bright-green blanched broccoli florets: Not only will they have an inviting look on your buffet station, but they also will be much nicer to eat.

Even at an omelet station that is high in demand and simple in nature you can raise the bar and make it something special. All it takes is the same approach to the other buffet stations you create, and with the same level of passion.

EGGS BENEDICT

There are differing accounts as to the origin of eggs Benedict. Some claim it started at the famed New York City restaurant Delmonico's when the Benedict's, frequent guests, asked the maître d'hotel to recommend something new or different for brunch. When asked what she might like, Mrs. Benedict suggested poached eggs on a toasted English muffin with a grilled slice of ham, hollandaise sauce, and a truffle on top.

Wherever it originated, eggs Benedict is a classic and a customer favorite. No brunch, Sunday morning breakfast, or brunch buffet would be complete without it. Tantalize your taste buds with modernized versions of this classic that are sure to please and will be the highlight of your breakfast buffet.

Classic Eggs Benedict | SERVES 8

INGREDIENTS

1 gal / 4 L   Water

4 fl oz / 125 ml   White wine vinegar

6 oz / 170 g   Unsalted butter, softened

4   English muffins, sliced in half

16 slices   Canadian bacon

8   Whole eggs

16 fl oz / 500 ml   Hollandaise Sauce*

Refer to Appendix A, "From the Chef's Pantry" (p. 199), for this signature recipe.

Method

1. Place the water and vinegar into a small stainless-steel rondo. Place the rondo over medium heat and bring the water to 185°F (85°C).

2. While the water is heating, spread 1/2 oz (15 g) of the softened butter onto each of the English muffin halves.

3. Place a large nonstick skillet over medium heat and add half of the buttered English muffins to the pan, butter side down. Allow the muffins to cook until lightly golden brown, approximately 2 minutes. Remove and repeat with the remaining muffin halves.

4. Once the water has reached the desired temperature, crack the eggs, one at a time, into the water. Poach the eggs until all of the white has cooked and the yolk is still liquid, approximately 5 minutes.

5. While the eggs are cooking, place a large skillet over medium heat and add the remaining soft butter. Add enough of the Canadian bacon to cover the bottom of the pan in a single layer. Brown the bacon on both sides, approximately 2 minutes each side. Remove and repeat until all the Canadian bacon is browned.

6. Place 1 English muffin onto each service plate.

7. Using tongs, place 2 slices of the browned Canadian bacon on top of each English muffin half.

8. Using a slotted spoon, remove the eggs from the water, one at a time, and place 1 egg on top of the bacon slices.

9. Top each egg with 1 oz (30 ml) of the hollandaise sauce and serve immediately.

Traditional eggs Benedict is the foundation for these inspired dishes. It is composed of a nicely toasted English muffin—toasting fully is the key to a great muffin—topped with Canadian bacon that has been seared in butter or grilled, a poached egg, and sauce hollandaise.

Lobster Eggs Benedict | SERVES 8

INGREDIENTS

1 lb / 450 g   Cooked Maine lobster meat, shelled and picked

6 oz / 170 g   Unsalted butter, softened

1 gal / 4 L   Water

4 fl oz / 125 ml   White wine vinegar

4   English muffins, sliced in half

8   Whole eggs

8 fl oz / 250 ml   Béarnaise Sauce*

*Refer to Appendix A, "From the Chef's Pantry" (p. 194), for this signature recipe.

Lobster Eggs Benedict is made with a toasted English muffin and poached lobster medallions topped with poached eggs, and finished with a vanilla bean hollandaise. A variation is to add bacon or pancetta to the lobster. The touch of vanilla bean in the hollandaise complements the sweet richness of the lobster.

Method

1. Slice the lobster tails into 16 equal pieces and place into an ovenproof dish.

2. Place 2 oz (60 g) of the softened butter into the pan with the lobster tails; cover tightly.

3. Place the dish into a preheated 250°F (120°C) oven and warm gently until heated through, approximately 10 minutes.

4. Place the water and vinegar into a small stainless-steel rondo. Place the rondo over medium heat and bring the water to 185°F (85°C).

5. While the water is heating, spread 1/2 oz (15 g) of the softened butter onto each of the English muffin halves.

6. Place a large nonstick skillet over medium heat and add half of the buttered English muffins, butter side down. Allow the muffins to cook until lightly golden brown, approximately 2 minutes on each side. Remove and repeat with the remaining muffin halves.

7. Once the water has reached the desired temperature, crack the eggs, one at a time, into the water. Poach the eggs until all of the white has cooked and the yolk is still liquid, approximately 5 minutes.

8. Place 1 English muffin onto each service plate.

9. Place 2 slices of the warmed lobster tail onto each English muffin half.

10. Using a slotted spoon, remove the eggs, one at a time, and place 1 egg on top of the lobster slices.

11. Top each egg with 1 fl oz (30 ml) of the béarnaise sauce and serve immediately.

Braised-Beef Short Ribs Eggs Benedict | SERVES 8

INGREDIENTS

1 lb / 450 g   Braised-beef short ribs*

16 fl oz / 500 ml   Braising liquid from the short ribs

1 gal / 4 L   Water

1/2 cup / 125 ml   White wine vinegar

4 oz / 115 g   Unsalted butter, softened

4   English muffins, sliced in half

8   Whole eggs

8 fl oz / 250 ml   Tomato Hollandaise Sauce*

Refer to Appendix A, "From the Chef's Pantry" (p, 195 and p. 199), for these signature recipes.

Method

1. Slice the short ribs into 16 equal pieces. Shingle the slices into an ovenproof dish and add the braising liquid.

2. Cover the dish and place into a preheated 300°F (150°C) oven and heat the short ribs through, approximately 15–20 minutes.

3. Place the water and vinegar into a small stainless-steel rondo. Place the rondo over medium heat and bring the water to 185°F (85°C).

4. While the water is heating, spread 1/2 oz (15 g) of the softened butter onto each English muffin half.

5. Place a large nonstick skillet over medium heat and add half of the buttered English muffins, butter side down. Allow the muffins to cook until lightly golden brown, approximately 2 minutes. Remove and repeat with the remaining muffin halves.

6. Once the water has reached the desired temperature, crack the eggs, one at a time, into the water. Poach the eggs until all of the white has cooked and the yolk is still liquid, approximately 5 minutes.

7. Place 1 English muffin onto each service plate.

8. Place 2 slices of warmed short ribs onto each English muffin half.

9. Using a slotted spoon, remove the eggs, one at a time, and place 1 egg on top of the short rib slices.

10. Top each egg with 1 oz (30 ml) of the tomato hollandaise and serve immediately.

Another version is Short Ribs Eggs Benedict. This version is full of flavor and texture and combines a variety of flavor profiles enjoyed by many guests. A toasted English muffin with braised short ribs of beef and poached eggs is topped with a hollandaise that has tomato and some of the braising sauce from the ribs folded into it.

Eggs Benedict Florentine (Spinach and Eggs Benedict) | SERVES 8

INGREDIENTS

1 gal / 4 L   Water

4 fl oz / 125 ml   White wine vinegar

4 oz / 115 g   Unsalted butter, softened

4   English muffins, sliced in half

8   Whole eggs

1 fl oz / 30 ml   Extra-virgin olive oil

1 Garlic clove, sliced

1 lb / 450 g   Fresh spinach, picked and washed

to taste   Kosher salt

8 fl oz / 250 ml   Hollandaise Sauce*

*Refer to Appendix A, "From the Chef's Pantry" (p. 199), for this signature recipe.

Eggs Benedict Florentine is a toasted English muffin topped with spinach (which has been sautéed in olive oil, a touch of garlic, and lardoons of bacon), a poached egg, and hollandaise sauce. Lemon is infused in the butter to complement the spinach and balance the richness of the sauce.

Method

1. Place the water and vinegar into a small stainless-steel rondo. Place the rondo over medium heat and bring the water to 185°F (85°C).

2. While the water is heating, spread 1/2 oz (15 g) of the softened butter onto each of the English muffin halves.

3. Place a large nonstick skillet over medium heat and add half of the buttered English muffins, butter side down. Allow the muffins to cook until lightly golden brown, approximately 2 minutes. Remove and repeat with the remaining muffin halves.

4. Once the water has reached the desired temperature, crack the eggs, one at a time, into the water. Poach the eggs until all of the white has cooked and the yolk is still liquid, approximately 5 minutes.

5. While the eggs are cooking, place a large skillet over medium heat and add the extra-virgin olive oil. Add the sliced garlic and cook gently for 2 minutes. Add the spinach and cook for an additional 2 minutes. Season to taste with kosher salt.

6. Place 1 English muffin onto each service plate.

7. Using tongs, place an equal amount of cooked spinach on top of each English muffin half.

8. Using a slotted spoon, remove the eggs, one at a time, and place 1 egg on top of the spinach.

9. Top each egg with 1 fl oz (30 ml) of the hollandaise sauce and serve immediately.

WAFFLES

Waffles with maple syrup or whipped cream and fruit is another alluring and classic breakfast choice. Using waffles as a sandwich base opens a completely new dimension to breakfast sandwiches. The slight sweetness and malt flavor of the waffle harmonize very well with a variety of food combinations, which lend themselves to the creation of new and innovative sandwiches for your breakfast buffet.

Steak, Egg, and Cheese Waffle Sandwich | SERVES 8

INGREDIENTS

4	Waffles,* 8 in. (20 cm)	
8	Filet mignons, 2 oz (60 g) each	
to taste	Kosher salt	
to taste	Fresh cracked black pepper	
4 oz / 115 g	Cheddar cheese, shredded	
2 oz / 60 g	Whole butter	
8	Whole eggs	

*Refer to Appendix A, "From the Chef's Pantry" (p. 205), for this signature recipe.

Here's a different twist on our Short Ribs Eggs Benedict. Egg fried in brown butter, seared filet mignon, and sharp cheddar cheese between waffles make for a savory version of steak, eggs, and cheese.

Method

1. Cut each waffle into 4 quarters. Place 8 quarters onto a half sheet pan.

2. Season the filet mignons with kosher salt and pepper and cook on a hot grill to the desired doneness.

3. Place 1 steak onto each of the waffle quarters.

4. Top each steak with an equal portion of shredded cheddar cheese.

5. Place a large nonstick skillet over medium heat and add 2 oz (60 g) of butter.

6. Once the butter begins to bubble, crack the eggs, one at a time, into the pan and fry each to the desired doneness. Season with kosher salt and black pepper.

7. Place 1 fried egg onto each of the waffle quarters topped with the steak and cheese.

8. Top each of the sandwiches with a second waffle quarter and place the pan into a preheated 300°F (150°C) oven; heat until the cheese is melted, approximately 3–5 minutes.

9. Remove from the oven and place onto a serving dish. Serve immediately.

Smoked Salmon and Egg Waffle Sandwich | SERVES 8

INGREDIENTS

4   Waffles,* 8 in. (20 cm)

8 oz / 250 g   Smoked salmon, sliced

16 slices   Roma tomatoes

4 oz / 115 g   Whole butter

8   Whole eggs

to taste   Kosher salt

to taste   Fresh cracked black pepper

8 fl oz / 250 ml   Béarnaise Sauce*

*Refer to Appendix A, "From the Chef's Pantry" (p. 194, 205), for these signature recipes.

Method

1. Cut each waffle into 4 quarters. Place 8 quarters onto a serving dish.

2. Place 1 oz (30 g) of sliced salmon onto each of the waffle quarters.

3. Place a large nonstick skillet over medium heat and add 2 oz (60 g) of butter.

4. Once the butter begins to bubble, crack the eggs, one at a time, into the pan and fry each to desired doneness. Season with kosher salt and black pepper.

5. Place 1 fried egg onto each of the waffle quarters topped with salmon.

6. Place 2 slices of Roma tomato onto each egg.

7. Top each sandwich with 1 fl oz (30 ml) of béarnaise sauce.

8. Place a second quarter of waffle atop each of the sandwiches. Serve immediately.

Waffles enclose this one-of-a-kind breakfast sandwich made of warm sliced tomatoes, béarnaise sauce, fried egg, and smoked salmon.

Applewood-Smoked Bacon, Cheese, and Egg Waffle Sandwich | SERVES 8

Fried egg, melted cheese, and peppery applewood-smoked bacon waffle sandwiches will give guests a reason to get up in the morning and be excited about breakfast. Remember, buffet offerings need to be simple, so that guests understand what they're getting, yet show flavor and be tempting.

INGREDIENTS

4	Waffles,* 8 in. (20 cm)
2 oz / 60 g	Whole butter
8	Whole eggs
to taste	Kosher salt
to taste	Fresh cracked black pepper
16	Applewood-smoked bacon slices, sliced and cooked
4 oz / 115 g	Cheddar cheese, shredded

*Refer to Appendix A, "From the Chef's Pantry" (p. 205), for this signature recipe.

Method

1. Cut each waffle into 4 quarters. Place 8 quarters onto a half sheet pan.

2. Place a large nonstick skillet over medium heat and add 2 oz (60 g) of whole butter.

3. Once the butter begins to bubble, crack the eggs, one at a time, into the pan and cook each to the desired doneness. Season with kosher salt and black pepper.

4. Place 1 fried egg onto each of the waffle quarters.

5. Top each egg with 2 slices of applewood-smoked bacon and an equal portion of shredded cheddar cheese.

6. Place a second piece of waffle on top of the cheese. Place the sheet pan into a preheated 300°F (150°C) oven and cook until the cheese is melted, approximately 5 minutes.

7. Remove the pan from the oven and place 1 sandwich onto each service plate. Serve immediately.

Canadian Bacon, Cheese, and Egg Waffle Sandwich | SERVES 8

INGREDIENTS

4	Waffles,* 8 in. (20 cm)
4 oz / 115 g	Whole butter
8	Canadian bacon, slices
8	Whole eggs
to taste	Kosher salt
to taste	Fresh cracked black pepper
4 oz / 115 g	Cheddar cheese, shredded

Refer to Appendix A, "From the Chef's Pantry" (p. 205), for this signature recipe.

Method

1. Cut each waffle into 4 quarters. Place 8 quarters onto a half sheet pan.

2. Place a large nonstick skillet over medium heat and add 2 oz (60 g) of butter.

3. Add the Canadian bacon slices and brown on both sides, approximately 2 minutes per side.

4. Remove the Canadian bacon from the pan and place 1 slice onto each of the waffle halves.

5. Place a large nonstick skillet over medium heat and add the remaining 2 oz (60 g) of butter.

6. Once the butter begins to bubble, crack the eggs, one at a time, into the pan and fry each to the desired doneness. Season with salt and pepper.

7. Place 1 fried egg onto each slice of Canadian bacon.

8. Top each egg with an equal portion of shredded cheddar cheese.

9. Place a second piece of waffle on top of the cheese and place the sheet pan into a preheated 300°F (150°C) oven and heat until the cheese is melted, approximately 5 minutes.

10. Remove from the oven and place 1 sandwich onto each service plate. Serve immediately.

Here, waffles serve as the wrap for fried eggs, creamy sharp cheddar cheese, and grilled Canadian bacon, bringing new taste sensations to the old favorite eggs, ham, and cheese.

Egg and Cheese Waffle Sandwich | SERVES 8

INGREDIENTS

4   Waffles,* 8 in. (20 cm)

2 oz / 60 g   Whole butter

8   Whole eggs

to taste   Kosher salt

to taste   Fresh cracked black pepper

4 oz / 115 g   Cheddar cheese, shredded

*Refer to Appendix A, "From the Chef's Pantry" (p. 205), for this signature recipe.

A breakfast sandwich can be as simple as eggs and cheese on a malted waffle, with variations limited only by your creativity. You might use mozzarella with warm tomatoes; or try a thin slice of brie with apple relish and egg. Using flavors that harmonize naturally is sure to make your sandwich creation a winner.

Method

1. Cut each waffle into 4 quarters. Place 8 quarters onto a half sheet pan.

2. Place a large nonstick skillet over medium heat and add 2 oz (60 g) of whole butter.

3. Once the butter begins to bubble, crack the eggs, one at a time, into the pan and fry each to the desired doneness. Season with salt and pepper.

4. Place 1 fried egg onto each of the waffle quarters.

5. Top each egg with an equal portion of shredded cheddar cheese.

6. Place a second piece of waffle on top of the cheese and place the sheet pan into a preheated 300°F (150°C) oven and heat until the cheese is melted, approximately 5 minutes.

7. Remove from the oven and place 1 sandwich onto each service plate. Serve immediately.

Sausage and Egg Waffle Sandwich | SERVES 8

INGREDIENTS

4	Waffles,* 8 in. (20 cm)
8	Breakfast sausages, cooked
2 oz / 60 g	Whole butter
8	Whole eggs
to taste	Kosher salt
to taste	Fresh cracked black pepper

Refer to Appendix A, "From the Chef's Pantry" (p. 205), for this signature recipe.

Method

1. Cut each waffle into 4 quarters. Place 8 quarters onto a half sheet pan.

2. Cut each sausage lengthwise into three slices. Place three slices onto each waffle quarter.

3. Place a second waffle quarter on top of the sliced sausage.

4. Place the half sheet pan into a preheated 300°F (150°C) oven for 3–5 minutes, until everything is heated through.

5. While the waffles and sausage are heating, place a large nonstick skillet over medium heat and add the whole butter.

6. Once the butter begins to bubble, crack the eggs, one at a time, into the pan and cook each to the desired doneness. Season with kosher salt and black pepper.

7. Remove the waffles from the oven and then take the top waffle from each stack.

8. Place 1 fried egg onto each of the heated waffles topped with sausage. Replace the top waffle and place onto a serving dish. Serve hot.

In this simple creation, waffles enclose fried eggs and sausage for a tasty treat. The spiciness of the sausage is offset by the slight sweetness of the waffles. The sausage links are sliced lengthwise for ease of eating and presentation.

LUNCH FOR ALL OCCASSIONS

*L*unch is more than a meal; often it's also a social or business event. Business meetings, conferences, and social get-togethers all commonly involve lunch. At hotels, clubs, and resorts, events like golf outings, tennis matches, swim meets, and camps—anything held during the midday hours—all typically include lunch.

The lunch buffet works especially well for people on the go and under time constraints. For groups attending a meeting or seminar, the lunch buffet can become a "working lunch" when it is set up in the room where the guests are gathered, and so can enjoy it at their convenience. Lunch buffets also can be an addition to à la carte venues that do a brisk lunch business, to help offset the à la carte menu and ease pressure on the kitchen and service staff.

Product freshness and high quality make the food on the buffet appealing and tempting to the guest. Smaller bowls and platters are refreshed more often, ensuring this objective is met.

When it comes to lunch, groups of all sizes, no matter the occasion, are best served buffet style, versus à la carte, primarily due to time restrictions. Guests, for the most part, do not want lunch to be as time-consuming as dinner. Typically, lunch breaks for any activity or event are scheduled with a time limit, to ensure that diners get back to the task or purpose at hand.

For the culinary team, lunch buffets are an opportunity to demonstrate how they can take traditional menu items and give them a new look and modern spin. Crisp, fresh-looking salads, tantalizing sandwiches, carved items, soups, and other fare become the foundation on which to build lunch buffets that not only are efficient time-wise, but tempting to the guest.

A buffet featuring smaller portions, such as petite sandwiches, sliders, and salads with a variety of toppings, gives the guest the option to dine lighter yet still enjoy flavorful

A new look to a traditional chef's salad promises to entice any salad aficionado. The glass vessel displays all salad items in a pleasing manner. Cipolini onions take the place of red onions; sliced skirt steak is an improvement over traditional roast beef. Small tomatoes are slightly roasted with olive oil for additional sweetness and flavor.

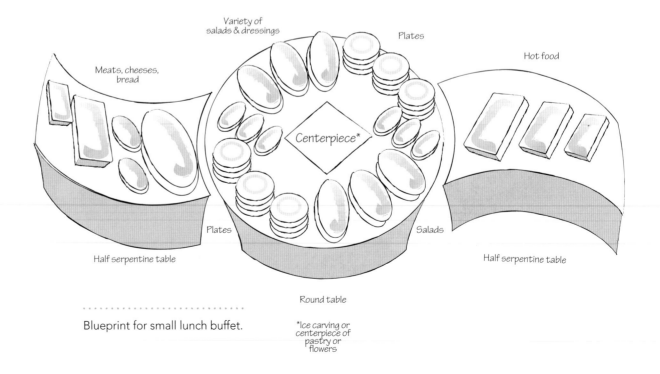

Blueprint for small lunch buffet.

fare. Additionally, a buffet in this style gives the guest the pleasure of sampling the many offerings featured on the buffet without overindulging.

This chapter showcases a spectacular lunch buffet that features mini sandwiches, burgers, and a chef's salad displayed in a completely new way. The Cobb salad buffet alone will ensure that you never look at this old favorite the same way again.

The standard lunch buffet offers a variety of simple salads, sliced meats, soups, hot selections, and a carver board with various accoutrements. Colorful but elegant glass highlights the buffet tables. Instead of chafers, a hot grill top is used, along with heatproof dishes that, along with heat lamps, give the food a fresh look. The dishes are refilled regularly throughout lunch to give all guests, no matter when they arrive, a feeling of value because they are receiving food that is cooked to order, rather than sitting all day in a steam bath heating unit.

This streamlined buffet takes up 8 feet of table space. Small sandwiches offer the guest choice, along with the option to eat lighter, while also limiting food waste. Sandwich combinations can be prepared on a variety of breads, for more choices, which are sure to leave a pleasing impression.

Flavors that marry well and naturally go together create the best dishes for buffet guests. Turkey, avocado, and tomatoes do just that. The key to this sandwich is fresh roasted turkey. For a real twist on flavor, add pepper-crusted bacon.

Turkey Avocado Sandwich | SERVES 8

INGREDIENTS

2	Avocados, ripe
3	Roma tomatoes
to taste	Kosher salt
to taste	Fresh cracked black pepper
1 head	Iceberg lettuce
8	Rolls of your choice, 2 oz (60 g) each
8 slices	Sharp white cheddar cheese
8 oz / 225 g	Turkey, sliced
2 fl oz / 60 ml	Avocado Mayonnaise*

Refer to Appendix A, "From the Chef's Pantry (p. 192), for this signature recipe.

Method

1. Cut avocado open and remove the skin. Reserve one quarter of each avocado for each sandwich.

2. Slice Roma tomatoes 1/8 in. (3 mm) thick and season with salt and pepper.

3. Remove core from iceberg lettuce; cut in quarters and wash.

4. Slice rolls horizontally, all the way through.

5. Place a slice of cheese on bottom portion of a roll, followed by a slice of turkey.

6. Slice each avocado quarter thin; place avocado slices on top of the turkey slice, followed by a slice of tomato, then lettuce.

7. Spread a thin layer of the mayonnaise on the cut side of each roll top and then place the roll top on top of the sandwich.

8. Secure each sandwich with a toothpick. Place the sandwiches on a platter and serve.

Mini Burger | SERVES 8

INGREDIENTS

8   Burgers, 2 oz (60 g) each

1   Spanish onion

2 tbsp / 30 ml   Whole butter

8 slices   Cheddar cheese, cut to the size of the rolls

8   Mini potato rolls

2 fl oz / 60 ml   House-made Ketchup*

8   Oven-Dried Grape Tomatoes*

to taste   Kosher salt

to taste   Fresh cracked black pepper

Refer to Appendix A, "From the Chef's Pantry" (p. 200 and p. 203), for these signature recipes.

Method

1. Grill the mini burgers to your liking and top with the sliced cheese.

2. Slice the onion thin, and sweat in whole butter.

3. Slice each potato roll horizontally, all the way through.

4. Place burger with cheese on the bottom portion of the roll.

5. Top each burger with onion and house-made ketchup.

6. Skewer a tomato with a sandwich pick and secure one on each sandwich, through the top bun of the burger, to hold everything together. Place the sandwiches on a platter and serve.

Mini burgers have become very popular in recent years. Healthy eating and nutritional concerns have created new market segments. Sinful foods in small bites and tasting portions enable those who watch what they eat a chance to indulge using a simple philosophy: everything in moderation.

Veal Milanese | SERVES 8

INGREDIENTS

16 oz / 450 g   Veal top round

1 cup / 225 g   Flour, seasoned with salt and pepper

16 fl oz / 450 ml   Egg wash, seasoned

1 cup / 225 g   Panko bread crumbs, finely ground

4 fl oz / 125 ml   Blended oil

8   Rolls of your choice, 2 oz (60 g) each

16   Olive Oil Tomato Petals*

2 cups / 450 g   Baby arugula

2 fl oz / 60 ml   Extra virgin olive oil

to taste   Kosher salt

to taste   Fresh cracked black pepper

1 tbsp / 15 ml   Lemon juice

1   Lemon

*Refer to Appendix A, "From the Chef's Pantry" (p. 202), for this signature recipe

A menu favorite that has stood the test of time becomes a small bite sandwich that is true buffet bliss. Because the veal is breaded, a light roll such as brioche or a nice olive soft roll is recommended.

Method

1. Slice the veal against the grain and pound into thin slices.

2. Dip each veal piece into flour, then egg wash, followed by the panko.

3. Pan-fry the veal slices in blended oil until cooked through.

4. Slice each roll horizontally, all the way through.

5. Place the cooked veal on bottom portion of the roll, followed by 2 pieces of olive oil tomato petals.

6. Season the arugula with salt, pepper, and lemon juice and place on top of the tomato pieces.

7. Cut the lemon into 12 quarters.

8. Skewer a lemon wedge with a sandwich pick and secure one on each sandwich, to hold them together. Place the sandwiches on a platter and serve.

Lobster Claw Sandwich | SERVES 8

INGREDIENTS

8	Lobster claws from 1.5 lb lobsters
1 gal / 4 L	Court Bouillon*
3	Roma tomatoes
to taste	Kosher salt
to taste	Fresh cracked black pepper
1 head	Baby Iceberg lettuce
1/2 cup / 120 ml	Mayonnaise
2 tsp / 10 ml	Old Bay Seasoning
1	Baguette
2 fl oz / 60 ml	Extra-virgin olive oil

*Refer to Appendix A, "From the Chef's Pantry" (p. 197), for this signature recipe.

Lobster lovers enjoy lobster in many ways. Often, the claw, an integral part of the lobster, gets passed by. This small sandwich stars the lobster claw and gives operations a nice use for this tasty meat.

Method

1. Blanch the lobster claws in court bouillon for 5-1/2 minutes. Place in an ice bath until cool.

2. Carefully remove the claw meat from the shells making sure to take out the cartilage.

3. Slice the Roma tomatoes, 1/8 in. (3 mm) thick, and season with salt and pepper.

4. Remove the core from the iceberg and cut the lettuce into quarters. Wash and dry.

5. Mix the mayonnaise with the old bay seasoning.

6. Slice the baguette horizontally, all the way through.

7. Spread the cut side of the baguette slices with the seasoned mayonnaise.

8. Place claw meat on bottom portion of the bread, followed by tomato slices.

9. Drizzle olive oil over the tomatoes; top the tomatoes with some lettuce, and place the top portion of baguette on top of the sandwich.

10. Secure 8 toothpicks along the top of the baguette. Cut the baguette into 8 portions, on a slight bias. Place the sandwiches on a platter and serve.

Eggplant Burger | SERVES 8

INGREDIENTS

1	Red bell pepper
to taste	Kosher salt
to taste	Fresh cracked black pepper
2 fl oz / 60 ml	Extra-virgin olive oil
1	Small eggplant
8 oz / 225 g	Flour, seasoned with salt and pepper
8 oz / 225 g	Italian bread crumbs
2 cups / 500 ml	Egg wash, seasoned
4 fl oz / 125 ml	Blended oil
8 oz / 225 g	Fresh mozzarella log: purchased
8	Rolls of your choice, 2 oz (60 g) each
2 cups / 500 g	Baby arugula
2 tsp / 10 ml	Lemon juice

Vegetarian choices are an important option on any menu, à la carte or buffet. This eggplant burger holds its own with other main sandwich items and is a winner even with meat eaters. A recommended roll would be a nice garlic or pesto roll.

Method

1. Season the red bell pepper with salt, pepper, and extra-virgin olive oil. Roast on an open flame until the skin blisters. Place in a bowl and cover with plastic wrap. Keep covered for 15 minutes.

2. Remove the roasted pepper from the bowl. Peel the skin away from the pepper and remove the seeds. Cut into julienne strips.

3. Slice the eggplant into 1/2-in. (1-cm) circles.

4. Dip each piece of eggplant into flour, then egg wash, followed by the bread crumbs. Pan-fry the breaded eggplant slices in blended oil until golden brown.

5. Slice each roll horizontally, all the way through.

6. Slice the mozzarella into 1-oz (30-g) portions; place one piece on each of the eggplant slices. Place the eggplant slices under a broiler or into a 350°F (175°C) oven for 1 to 2 minutes, until the cheese melts.

7. Place an eggplant slice on the bottom portion of a roll, followed by slices of the julienne red pepper.

8. Season the arugula with salt, pepper, and lemon juice and place on top of the roasted pepper.

9. Secure each sandwich top with a sandwich pick. Place the sandwiches on a platter and serve.

Tomato Mozzarella Sandwich | SERVES 8

INGREDIENTS

8 oz / 225 g Fresh mozzarella log: (purchased)

8 Rolls of your choice, 2 oz (60 g) each

8 Roasted Roma tomatoes

1 head Baby Iceberg lettuce

2 fl oz / 60 ml Pesto mayonnaise *

to taste Kosher salt

to taste Fresh cracked black pepper

For pesto mayonnaise, mix three part mayonnaise with one part pesto.

Method

1. Slice the mozzarella into 1-oz (30-g) portions.

2. Slice each roll horizontally, all the way through.

3. Remove the core from the lettuce and cut lettuce into quarters and wash.

4. Place a roasted tomato on the bottom portion of each roll.

5. Top each tomato with a slice of mozzarella, then lettuce.

6. Spread a layer of mayonnaise on the cut side of each roll top and then place the roll on top of the sandwich.

7. Secure the sandwiches with toothpicks before placing them on a platter to serve.

A customer favorite, from pizza to the caprese salad, mozzarella and tomato are enjoyed by many. The twist of this petite sandwich is that the tomatoes are roasted. The combination of the mozzarella, sweet roasted tomato, and pesto is a flavorful winner. For the roll try a nice semolina or brioche so the contents of the sandwich remain the stars.

CHAPTER FOUR

COMPOSITION OF FLAVORFUL SALADS

*S*alads have come a long way, in both presentation and menu design, since the ancient Romans and Greeks enjoyed a variety of dishes composed of raw vegetables dressed with oil, vinegar, and herbs (the word "salad" comes from the Latin sal, for salt). Seasonal flavors, ethnic influences, changing tastes, and creative interpretations have all played roles in spicing up classic salads for buffet fare—all for the better. Salads today may be substantial accompaniments to main plates on a buffet, or even comprise a whole buffet themselves, with a full range of meat, fish, poultry, and vegetarian options.

Salads derive their flavor primarily from the dressing, marinade, or vinaigrette used to complement the salad ingredients. Even when the items in the salad are spiced or have a full flavor profile of their

own, the appropriate dressing enhances an already tasty salad. Simply put, a delicious dressing or vinaigrette can make a bowl of tossed greens come alive.

Salads prepared for a buffet service do, however, present more of a challenge, as compared to the composition of à la carte salads. They are made in larger quantities, and may sit on the table for longer periods of time, whereas an à la carte salad is tossed or prepared to order, then immediately sent to the table. The key to successful buffet salads is to prepare them component style. That is: prepare and season all items so they are ready to go; then, as the salad is needed for the buffet, mix the components, garnish the salad, and place it on the buffet. This process has two important benefits: First, the salad always looks fresh and is full of flavor; second, the leftover components can be used for the fresh production of salads for the next buffet.

A specialty self-serve buffet station.

Hot Food Buffet

Pressed Watermelon Salad with Arugula and Goat Cheese | SERVES 6

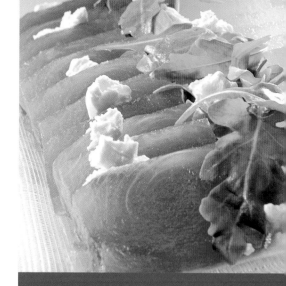

INGREDIENTS

1   Red watermelon, small, seedless

1   Yellow watermelon, small, seedless

4 fl oz / 125 ml   Tarragon and basil-infused simple syrup*

8 oz / 225 g   Baby arugula, cleaned

as needed   Extra-virgin olive oil

as needed   Sea salt

6 oz / 170 g   Quality goat cheese

For syrup, place 1/2 cup water, 1/2 cup sugar. 5 basil leaves, and 8 tarragon leaves in a saucepan and bring to boil. Let steep 15 minutes and then strain.

Method

1. Using a serrated knife, remove the rind from both watermelons.

2. Cut a 1-in. (2.5-cm) thick slice from each watermelon. Place each slice into a large Cryovac® bag. Pour an equal amount of the herbed simple syrup into the two Cryovac® bags and seal them tightly. Place into the refrigerator overnight to marinate.

3. The next day, remove the watermelon from both bags and trim to the desired shape. Cut each piece of watermelon into 1/4-in. (6-mm) slices and arrange on a service platter.

4. Place the arugula into a stainless-steel bowl and toss lightly with extra-virgin olive oil and sea salt.

5. Lay the dressed arugula over the sliced watermelon.

6. Using your hands, gently crumble the goat cheese over the salad. Serve immediately.

Pressed yellow and red watermelon is complemented by goat cheese and arugula, more proof that simplicity combined with elegance is the perfect match in food display for a buffet.

A salad of roasted pears, avocado, and lump crab is an ideal combination for autumn. The pears are poached in butter, tossed with lump crab meat, and finished with a spiced dressing. The dressing's flavor profiles of acid and fall spices break down the rich fat of the avocado. Fried sage leaves and dried pear chips garnish the salad.

Butter-Poached Pear, Avocado, and Jumbo Lump Crab Meat, with Spiced Cider Vinaigrette | SERVES 6

INGREDIENTS

Dressing

4 fl oz / 125 ml	Apple cider
1	Star anise
1	Cinnamon stick
2	Cloves
1	Allspice berry
4 fl oz / 125 ml	Apple cider vinegar
1/2 tsp / 2 ml	Dijon mustard
16 fl oz / 500 ml	Grapeseed oil
as needed	Kosher salt
as needed	Fresh cracked pepper

Salad

2 lb / 900 g	Unsalted butter
4	Anjou pears
1–1/2 lb / 675 g	Jumbo lump crab meat
3	Hass avocados, ripe
12	Fried sage leaves*
12	Dried pear chips

For fried sage leaves, select nice, whole leaves, dust lightly with flour, and deep fry for 15-20 seconds.

Method

1. Place apple cider into a small stainless-steel saucepan and add star anise, cinnamon, cloves, and allspice. Bring to a simmer over medium heat; remove once cider begins to boil. Steep 10 minutes. Strain; chill completely.

2. Place the chilled, steeped cider, vinegar, and mustard into a blender and blend on high speed for 1 minute. Reduce speed and slowly add grapeseed oil. Season vinaigrette with kosher salt and pepper. Reserve for service.

3. Place the butter into a medium saucepan and put over medium heat until the butter is melted.

4. While the butter is melting, peel the pears, cut into 6 equal pieces, and remove the cores.

5. Cook butter until it begins to brown. Add the pear pieces and continue to cook until they are tender. Remove pears from butter and allow to cool to room temperature. Reserve the brown butter in the refrigerator for later use.

6. Place the cooled pears into a large stainless-steel bowl and add the crab meat.

7. Cut avocados in half; remove pits. Using a melon baller, scoop out the avocado; add to the pears and crab meat.

8. Add enough dressing to coat; then gently toss pear mixture. Season to taste with salt and pepper.

9. Arrange the dressed pear mixture on a service plate. Garnish the salad with fried sage leaves and dried pear chips.

10. Finish the salad with a drizzle of the spiced dressing. Serve immediately.

Roasted Yellow Beets and Endive Salad with Orange Segments, Toasted Almonds, and Lavender Dressing | SERVES 6

INGREDIENTS

Dressing

6	Oranges
1 tsp / 5 ml	Lavender, dried
1 tsp / 5 ml	Mustard
2 fl oz / 60 ml	Champagne vinegar
24 fl oz / 750 ml	Grapeseed oil
as needed	Kosher salt
as needed	Fresh cracked pepper
as needed	Extra-virgin olive oil

Salad

6	Yellow beets, roasted and peeled
3 heads	Red endive, cleaned and picked
6 heads	Mâche, cleaned
1 cup / 250 g	Sliced almonds, toasted
as needed	Edible flowers, washed

This is an excellent example of a component salad. Sliced yellow beets are the foundation for orange sections, red endive, arugula, and lavender dressing. Toasted almonds and edible flowers ensure this salad looks as good as it tastes.

Method

1. Using a small knife, remove the outer skin from one orange, being sure to remove all of the white pith. Separate the segments and place into a stainless-steel container.

2. When all the segments have been removed, squeeze the juice from the remaining five oranges into a small stainless-steel saucepan.

3. Place the saucepan with the juice over medium heat until it is reduced by half.

4. Remove the juice from the stove and add the dried lavender. Allow to steep for 5 minutes.

5. Strain the juice into a stainless-steel container. Chill completely.

6. Place chilled juice, mustard, and vinegar into blender on high speed for 1 minute. Reduce to medium speed; slowly add the grapeseed oil. Season dressing to taste with salt and pepper. Reserve for service.

7. Slice beets thinly using a mandoline or very sharp knife; arrange slices in a single layer on a service plate.

8. Lightly drizzle the beets with extra-virgin olive oil, followed by a sprinkle of kosher salt.

9. Arrange endive leaves, mâche, and orange segments on top of the beets. Drizzle dressing over salad and garnish with toasted almonds and edible flowers. Serve at room temperature.

This unique salad features strawberries, frisée, candied pecans, and pressed avocado. Strawberry champagne dressing complements the flavors on the platter. It is drizzled over the salad prior to placing on the buffet.

Pressed Avocado, Strawberries, Candied Pecans, and Frisée with Strawberry Champagne Dressing | SERVES 6

INGREDIENTS

Dressing

1 qt / 250 ml	Overripe strawberries, chopped
4 fl oz / 125 ml	Quality champagne vinegar
1 tsp / 5 ml	Fresh basil, chopped
1/2 tsp / 2 ml	Mustard
24 fl oz / 750 ml	Grapeseed oil
as needed	Kosher salt
as needed	Fresh cracked pepper

Salad

6	Hass avocados, ripe
6	Limes, juiced
as needed	Kosher salt
as needed	Fresh cracked black pepper
24	Fresh strawberries
6 heads	Frisée, cleaned
24 pieces	Candied pecans
30 pieces	Strawberry slices, dried

Method

1. To prepare the dressing, place the chopped overripe strawberries, vinegar, mustard, and basil into a blender and blend on high speed for 30 seconds.

2. Reduce the blender speed to medium and slowly add the grapeseed oil.

3. Once all the oil is incorporated, turn off the blender and season dressing to taste with kosher salt and fresh cracked pepper. Pulse in blender one to two times after adding seasonings.

4. Pour dressing into a squeeze bottle. Reserve for service.

5. Cut the avocados in half and remove pits and outer skin. Place the avocado halves into a stainless-steel bowl and add the lime juice. Lightly season with kosher salt and fresh cracked pepper.

6. Place the avocado halves into a large Cryovac® bag and seal tightly.

7. Using a rolling pin, gently roll the avocados into an even sheet, approximately 1/4-in. (6-mm) thick.

8. Place the avocado sheet onto a flat pan and then into the freezer for at least 1 hour.

9. At time of service, remove the avocado sheet from the freezer and cut into the desired shape and lay on a service platter. Allow the avocado to sit for about 10 minutes.

10. Cut the fresh strawberries into quarters and arrange attractively on the avocado sheet.

11. Place the frisée into a bowl and toss lightly with the strawberry dressing.

12. Arrange the dressed frisée on the service plate.

13. Garnish the salad with the candied pecans and dried strawberry slices.

14. Finish the salad with a light drizzle of the strawberry dressing. Serve immediately.

Potato and Lentil Salad with Roasted Duck Breast | SERVES 8

Here is another recipe that proves even the simplest of flavors can be expressed in an elegant and attractive manner. This salad of lentils, potatoes, and duck breast with marinated celery comes alive in this torte-like presentation sure to enhance any lunch or dinner buffet.

INGREDIENTS

1 tbsp / 15 ml Unsalted butter	as needed Fresh cracked pepper
1 Carrot, finely diced	8 Large Yukon gold potatoes, peeled
1 Small white onion, small dice	2 tsp / 10 ml Salt
1 Garlic clove, sliced thin	1 tbsp / 15 ml Cider vinegar
1 Celery stalk, finely diced	2 tbsp / 30 ml Creole mustard
2 cups / 500 g Green lentils	2 500 Hard-cooked eggs, chopped
1 qt / 1 L Chicken stock	16 fl oz / 500 ml Mayonnaise
1 Bay leaf	as needed Extra-virgin olive oil
1 tsp / 5 ml Fresh thyme, chopped	3 Duck breast, cooked
as needed Kosher salt	1 cup / 250 g Celery leaves, cleaned

Method

1. Place a medium saucepan over medium heat, add the butter, and begin to melt.

2. Add the carrot, onion, garlic, and celery and cook over medium heat, stirring often, until the vegetables have softened.

3. Add the green lentils and continue to cook, while stirring, for an additional 2 minutes.

4. Add the chicken stock and bay leaf and bring to a simmer.

5. Cook the lentils until all the stock has been absorbed and the lentils are tender, about 16 minutes.

6. Remove the lentils from the stove and add the chopped thyme. Season to taste with kosher salt and pepper.

7. Spread the lentils out on a flat tray. Cool to room temperature and reserve.

8. Cut the potatoes into 1/2-in. (1-cm) pieces and place into a medium saucepan.

9. Cover with 1 in. (2.5 cm) cold water and add 2 tsp (15 g) of salt.

10. Place over medium heat and bring to a boil. Cook the potatoes until they are tender.

11. Once the potatoes are tender, remove from the water and place into a stainless-steel bowl and allow to cool for 10 minutes.

12. Add the cider vinegar, mustard, chopped egg, and mayonnaise. Toss lightly to combine. Season to taste with salt and pepper. Allow to cool completely and reserve for service.

13. At time of service, lightly oil a cake ring with extra-virgin olive oil. Place the cake ring onto a service plate.

14. Place half of the potato salad into the oiled ring; gently push into place evenly, to fill the mold.

15. Lay half of the lentils on top of the potato salad and spread out evenly.

16. Add the remaining potato salad on top of the lentils and press firmly into place.

17. Add the remaining lentils on top of the potato salad layer and press firmly into place.

18. Using a sharp knife, cut the duck breast into even slices and shingle over the layer of lentils.

19. Toss the celery leaves lightly with extra-virgin olive oil, salt, and pepper.

20. Place the seasoned celery leaves into the center of the sliced duck breast.

21. At time of service, gently remove the cake ring and serve immediately.

Orzo Salad with Grilled Vegetables and Roasted Cipollini Onions | SERVES 6

This display of orzo salad has the wow factor. A first, flavorful layer of orzo is arranged on the bottom of the serving platter and covered with thin beet slices. A second layer of orzo is wrapped in grilled zucchini and topped with roasted cipollinis and olives.

Orzo has never looked so good, far surpassing its commonplace presentation in a large bowl, sprinkled with parsley.

INGREDIENTS

1 lb / 450 g	Orzo pasta, cooked al dente	
1 cup / 250 g	Carrot, finely diced and cooked	
1/2 cup / 125 g	Celery, finely diced	
1/4 cup / 60 g	Parsley, chopped fine	
1 tsp / 5 ml	Cider vinegar	
1/3 cup / 80 ml	Extra-virgin olive oil	
2 Tbsp / 30 g	Dijon mustard	
1 cup / 375 ml	Mayonnaise	

2	Zucchini
2	Yellow squash
as needed	Extra-virgin olive oil
as needed	Kosher salt
as needed	Fresh cracked pepper
2	Golden beets, roasted and peeled, sliced thin
20	Cipollini onions, peeled and roasted
24	Picholine olives, no pits
as needed	Fried parsley leaves*

For fried parsley leaves, select large parsley leaves, dry well, and deep fry for 5 to 10 seconds.

Method

1. Place the cooked orzo into a stainless-steel bowl and add the carrot, celery, parsley, vinegar, mustard, olive oil, and mayonnaise. Stir gently with a wooden spoon to combine.

2. Season to taste with kosher salt and pepper. Cover with plastic wrap and reserve in the refrigerator for service.

3. Using a knife, trim the ends of the zucchini and yellow squash.

4. Slice the zucchini and squash lengthwise into 1/4-in. (6-mm) thick slices.

5. Season the slices with extra-virgin olive oil, salt, and pepper.

6. Place the slices onto a preheated grill and cook for 2 minutes on each side.

7. Remove the slices from the grill and allow to cool completely.

8. Lightly coat a medium cake ring with extra-virgin olive oil and place onto a service plate.

9. Put half of the orzo salad into the ring and press firmly into place.

10. Arrange a single layer of the roasted beet slices over the orzo salad

11. Lightly oil a small cake ring and place it on top of the layer of roasted beets.

12. Line the inside of the small cake ring with the grilled vegetables, being sure to leave at least 1 in. (2.5 cm) of grilled vegetables hanging over the top of the cake ring.

13. Place the remaining orzo salad into the small cake ring and fold the extra grilled vegetables over the top of the salad.

14. Place the roasted Cipollini onions and olives on top of the salad.

15. At time of service, gently remove the two cake rings and garnish the salad with the fried parsley leaves. Serve immediately.

Traditional tuna salad Niçoise, when adapted to a buffet setting, can become a unique and distinctive presentation. Creativity, expressed sensibly, is the key here. Slices of egg, tuna, potatoes, and roasted tomatoes, garnished with an olive, are placed on top of French green beans that have been laid on the platter in alternating directions.

The creative elements are up to you. Just be sure that when you deviate from a classical presentation or recipe, you name it "in the style of" such as this dish: "Niçoise style."

Tuna Salad, Niçoise Style | SERVES 8

INGREDIENTS

Vinaigrette

1/4 cup / 60 ml   High-quality cider vinegar

1/4 cup / 60 ml   Fresh lime juice

1 tbsp / 5 ml   Quality Dijon-style mustard

2 tsp / 10 ml   Stone-ground mustard

1 cup / 250 ml   Extra-virgin olive oil

2   Garlic cloves, minced

1   Shallot, small, very small dice

3 cups / 675 ml   Flat-leaf parsley leaves, loosely packed

3/4 cup / 175 ml   Mixture of tarragon and fresh chervil leaves, loosely packed

to taste   Sea salt

to taste   Freshly ground black pepper

Salad

2 lb / 900 g   Fresh tuna

1 tbsp / 15 ml   Extra-virgin olive oil, for rubbing on the tuna

as needed   Course sea salt

as needed   Freshly ground black pepper

20   White anchovy fillets

2 lb / 900 g   Yukon gold potatoes, medium size

12   Roma tomatoes

2 tbsp / 30 ml   Olive oil

1 lb / 450 g   French green beans, trimmed and blanched

8   Farm eggs, hard-cooked, peeled and sliced

1 cup / 225 g   Niçoise olives

Sprigs of parsley and chervil, for garnish

Method

To prepare the vinaigrette:

1. In a large bowl, whisk together the vinegar, lime juice, and the mustards. In a thin stream, slowly whisk in the extra-virgin olive oil, to emulsify the mixture. Stir in the garlic and the shallots.

2. Mince the parsley and add it, with the tarragon and chervil, to the dressing, mixing well.

3. Season to taste with sea salt and pepper.

To make the salad:

4. Rinse the tuna, pat it dry, and refrigerate it until just before cooking.

5. When ready to cook, rub the tuna with oil and season with sea salt and pepper.

6. In a hot cast-iron or heavy-bottomed pan, sear the tuna until lightly golden, 3–4 minutes.

7. Carefully turn the tuna and cook until it is golden on the other side and opaque through, an additional 3–4 minutes. Let cool and reserve.

8. Drain the anchovies and pat them dry.

9. Bring a medium pot of salted water to a boil; add the potatoes. Cook until they are just tender, about 12–18 minutes. Drain and let cool.

10. Slice each potato into about 1/4-in. (6-mm) slices.

11. Cut each tomato in half and toss with the olive oil. Place on a rack and roast in a 350°F (175°C) oven for 8 minutes. Let cool.

12. For a modern presentation, on a platter or square plate, make a bed of the trimmed and blanched French green beans, lining them up to form alternating squares to cover the plate. Set up the platter in four sections. On one section, place the sliced tuna; on another, the sliced hard-cooked egg; on the third, the roasted tomatoes; and on the last section, the sliced potatoes. In each tomato half, place an olive; and down the middle of the plate the anchovies. Dress the salad with the vinaigrette, and garnish with micro greens, if desired.

CHAPTER FIVE

DINNERS WITH FLAIR

Dinner buffets present more of a challenge than any other type of buffet, for one primary reason: The menu is composed mostly of hot offerings. Unlike cold platters and salads that can be given a decorative touch in the form of garnishes, and can look fresh longer, hot food, for the most part, must stand on its own, and its appearance can deteriorate over time.

Presenting hot food on a buffet in large batches and in traditional chafers can be effective when serving large numbers of guests at a quick rate of turnover. Whether using the traditional method of service or some of the new buffet service vessels shown in this chapter, the rules are the same:

- Batch cook, timed in accordance with your buffet timeline. This makes it possible to keep all hot food looking fresh and appetizing for longer periods of time.

- Use the menu accoutrements that accompany the main item as a functional garnish and for ease of service, regardless of the vessel being used to display your food. I call this the à la carte approach.

- Use knife cuts effectively. They are important to highlight the presentation of vegetables—and all food—as a functional garnish.

- Enhance food flavor, adorn the presentation, and increase guest satisfaction, by using herbs, oils, and a variety of salts, sauces, dried fruits, and vegetables, along with fried items, to name a few.

- Focus on the layout of the food. A good layout is essential to maintaining the fresh, modern approach of the food and, in turn, the buffet.

- Shingle food to increase the number of portions in the vessels and add style to the presentation.

- Write a hot food buffet menu that features sensible food, keeping in mind that certain foods do not hold or present well on a buffet.

The display of the hot food buffet recipes in this chapter take an à la carte plating approach. Regardless of the venue, numbers, and type of service, the presentation of cuisine should adhere to the same high standards; likewise, the approach should be consistent. Quality must always be your first, and foremost, goal. You want to exceed the guest's expectations and make the food look as inviting as possible. This level of achievement, even in a buffet setting, is possible, regardless of the resources or equipment you have on hand. The buffet, unlike à la carte service, is an opportunity to tempt, to invite the guest in—to say, in effect, "Look at how good our food is." You want to make it challenging for the guest to choose what to eat, because everything looks so appetizing. A great buffet does this, and more.

A complete buffet with various table shapes and zoning system for large number of guests.

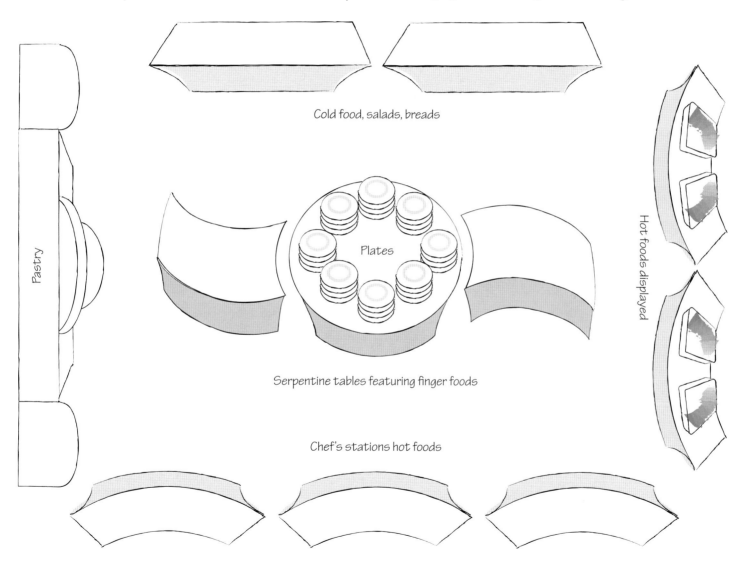

Cold food, salads, breads

Pastry

Plates

Hot foods displayed

Serpentine tables featuring finger foods

Chef's stations hot foods

Baked Sole Fillet, Roasted Zucchini, Squash, and Bread Sauce | SERVES 6

This recipe takes fillet of sole—a customer favorite—and finishes it with a classic bread sauce. The preparation of the sole gives it tantalizing flavor, while the unique modern presentation maintains the integrity of the fish, which is a key in buffet presentation. The sauce, thickened by the bread, has intense flavor depth thanks to the veal stock and the anchovies.

INGREDIENTS

1	Zucchini, large		1	Bay leaf
1	Yellow squash, large		pinch	Nutmeg
as needed	Extra-virgin olive oil		4	Black peppercorns
as needed	Kosher salt		2 oz / 60 g	Unsalted butter, cold, diced
as needed	Fresh cracked pepper		4 fl oz / 125 ml	Veal stock
6 sprigs	Fresh thyme, picked		3 tbsp / 45 ml	Heavy cream
6	Sole fillets, 5 oz (150 g) each		1/2 cup / 125 ml	Bread cubes, toasted
6 tsp / 30 ml	Unsalted butter		2	Anchovies, chopped fine
1	Onion, small		2 tbsp / 30 ml	Extra-virgin olive oil
3	Cloves		6	Tempura-fried thyme*
8 fl oz / 250 ml	Milk		6	Candied Leeks**

*To prepare, take whole sprigs of thyme, dip in your favorite tempura batter, and fry lightly.

**Refer to Appendix A, "From the Chef's Pantry" (p. 196), for this signature recipe.

Method

1. Using a knife, trim the ends off the zucchini and yellow squash. Slice each lengthwise, into thin strips. Place all strips into a bowl and toss with extra-virgin olive oil, salt, and pepper.

2. Lay seasoned strips onto a sheet pan with a roasting rack; place into a preheated 350°F (175°C) oven; and roast until they are tender, approximately 5 minutes. Remove from oven and cool. Reserve for later use.

3. Place 6 squares of aluminum foil that measure 8 in. x 8 in. (20 cm x 20 cm) onto your work surface. Rub each sheet lightly with extra-virgin olive oil and sprinkle with salt, pepper, and thyme.

4. Place 1 portion of fish, skin side up, in the center of each foil square.

5. Season the skin side of the fish with salt and pepper. Place 1 tsp (5 ml) of butter onto each portion of fish.

6. Roll each portion of fish in the foil, to form a log, and secure the ends of the foil tightly. Place into the refrigerator until time of service.

7. Stud the onion with the cloves and place into a medium stainless-steel saucepan.

8. Add the milk, bay leaf, nutmeg, and peppercorns and slowly bring to a boil over medium-low heat.

9. As soon as the milk begins to simmer, remove it from the heat and cover with plastic wrap. Allow the milk mixture to sit covered for 30 minutes.

10. Strain the milk into a clean stainless-steel pan and add the butter, veal stock, and cream. Return to medium heat and bring to a simmer.

11. Once it has reached a simmer, reduce the heat to low and whisk in the toasted bread cubes and anchovies; continue to stir until the sauce has thickened.

12. Pour the sauce into a blender, turn on medium, and slowly add the 2 tbsp (30 ml) of extra-virgin olive oil.

13. Strain sauce through a fine sieve. Season to taste with salt and pepper. Pour sauce into a squeeze bottle and reserve at room temperature for service.

14. At time of service, place the wrapped fish into a preheated 325°F (160°C) oven. Cook for 7–10 minutes, or until fish reaches an internal temperature of 140°F (60°C).

15. Remove from the oven and allow to rest while you prepare the service dish.

16. To plate, line the bottom of the service dish with the roasted slices of zucchini and yellow squash. Place dish into a preheated 325°F (160°C) oven for 3 minutes, to warm the vegetables.

17. Unwrap the fish and arrange the portions on top of the warmed vegetable slices. Spoon some of the sauce onto each portion of fish. Garnish with tempura-fried thyme and candied leeks. Serve hot.

Pan-Seared Salmon, Braised Sauerkraut, Pork Belly, and Mustard Butter Sauce | SERVES 6

INGREDIENTS

8 fl oz / 250 ml	White wine
8 fl oz / 250 ml	Champagne vinegar
2 sprigs	Thyme
1	Shallot, sliced
1 tbsp / 15 ml	Heavy cream
1 lb / 450 g	Unsalted butter, very cold, diced
4 oz / 120 g	Whole-grain mustard
as needed	Kosher salt
as needed	Fresh cracked pepper

6	Salmon mignons, 4 oz (120 g) each
3 tbsp / 45 ml	Canola oil
3 cups / 750 g	Sauerkraut
2 tbsp / 30 ml	Butter
1	Shallot, minced
1/4 cup / 30 ml	Apple juice
6	Cooked pork bellies, sliced, 2 oz (60 g) each
as needed	Chives, snipped

Method

1. Put the white wine, vinegar, shallots, and thyme into a 1-qt (1-L) saucepan and place over medium heat. Simmer until almost all the liquid has evaporated.

2. Add the heavy cream and bring back to a simmer.

3. Remove from the heat and slowly whisk in the cold butter until it is incorporated.

4. Strain through a fine sieve. Add the whole-grain mustard and whisk to incorporate. Season to taste with salt and pepper. Reserve in a warm place for service.

5. Place a heavy-bottom sauté pan over medium heat and allow to preheat for 3–5 minutes.

6. Season the salmon mignons with salt and pepper. Add canola oil to the preheated pan.

7. Once the oil begins to smoke, add the salmon mignons, skin side up, to the pan and cook until golden brown. Turn the salmon over and continue to cook until the salmon is medium. Remove from the pan and reserve in a warm place for service.

8. In the same pan, add the butter and shallots. Cook for 1 minute then add the sauerkraut and apple juice. Sauté for 3 to 5 minutes then reserve.

9. In a 360°F (180°C) oven, heat the pork belly through until hot, about 5 minutes.

10. Arrange the pork slices along the sides of a serving dish and lay the salmon mignons over the sauerkraut.

11. Spoon the mustard sauce over the salmon mignons. Sprinkle with chopped chives and serve with boiled potatoes and glazed carrots. Serve immediately.

When in France I studied with a chef who owned a choucroute (sauerkraut) restaurant. What was unusual about this establishment was that it featured mainly seafood. Sauerkraut was seasoned and prepared to complement the type of fish with which it was to be served. It was there that I learned to appreciate this unique pairing of foods, which produces flavors that make memorable meals.

Not only is this salmon dish a great buffet item—it holds well for service—but also it has great color and, most important, is one of the most enjoyable dishes you can eat.

Tomato Tatin | SERVES 6

INGREDIENTS

12 Vine ripe tomatoes, peeled and pulp removed, cut into petals

2 tbsp / 30 ml Sugar

1/3 cup / 80 ml Extra-virgin olive oil

1 tbsp / 15 ml Sugar

as needed Kosher salt

as needed Fresh cracked pepper

1 cup / 250 ml Ricotta cheese

2 tbsp / 30 ml Heavy cream

2 tbsp / 30 ml Unsalted butter

1 tbsp / 15 ml Olive oil

12 oz / 340 g Red onion, julienned

1 tbsp / 15 ml Brown sugar

3 fl oz / 90 ml Red wine

3 fl oz / 90 ml Red wine vinegar

1 tsp / 5 ml Tarragon, chopped

6 Puff pastry circles, 4.5-in. (12-cm) diameter

1 Whole egg, whipped

3 cups / 500 g Frisée, cleaned

as needed Extra-virgin olive oil

This has been a buffet item on my menus for many years. It is simple at its core and close to a perfect dish to feature on your buffets. Buttery pastry for texture, creamy warm cheese, sweet tomatoes, and onions, all finished with pesto, make for a perfect complement to the tatin.

Method

1. Place tomato petals into stainless-steel bowl; toss with sugar and extra-virgin olive oil. Season lightly with salt and pepper.

2. Sprinkle sugar between the six 4-in. (10-cm) tart pans. Divide the tomato petals among the tart pans.

3. Place tart pans into 250°F (120°C) oven; bake 1 hour. Remove; reserve at room temperature.

4. In a stainless-steel bowl, combine the ricotta, heavy cream, and 3 tbsp (45 ml) of the pesto; combine well. Season to taste with salt and pepper. Reserve.

5. Place a large sauté pan over medium-high heat and add the unsalted butter and olive oil. Add the onion and cook for 5 minutes, or until the onion begins to caramelize.

6. Add the brown sugar, wine, and vinegar to the onion and cook until most of the liquid is evaporated. Remove from the heat and add the tarragon. Season with salt and pepper. Reserve.

7. Place puff pastry circles onto lined baking sheet and brush with whipped egg. Cover with second sheet of parchment and 1 sheet pan. Weigh down top pan with 3 additional sheet pans. Refrigerate 20 minutes prior to baking.

8. Place into a preheated 400°F (205°C) oven and cook for 5 minutes. Remove from the oven; remove extra pans and reserve at room temperature.

9. Divide onion mixture evenly among pans. Top onion with an equal portion of ricotta mixture.

10. Lay a pastry circle on top of cheese. Place tart pans into preheated 350°F (175°C) oven. Bake until pastry is golden brown and tart is hot all the way through, approximately 10–12 minutes. Remove from the oven and place 1 tart, pastry side down, onto each of the service vessels.

11. Toss frisée lightly with salt, pepper, and olive oil. Place an equal portion onto each tart. Serve warm.

Roasted Lamb Loin, Confit Shoulder, and Braised Shank Cassoulet | SERVES 6

People tend to enjoy lamb more when they dine out than at home. This buffet lamb dish requires three types of preparation, which make it a truly special menu item for your buffet. Prime-cut roasted lamb loin is teamed with confit and braised lamb with beans, for a winning combination.

INGREDIENTS

Lamb Shoulder

1 cup / 250 ml   Brown sugar

1 cup / 250 ml   Kosher salt

1–1/2 lb / 675 g   Lamb shoulder

as needed   Kosher salt

as needed   Fresh cracked pepper

2 qt / 2 L   Olive oil

2   Garlic cloves, smashed

1 sprig   Rosemary

2   Shallots

Confit

1 tbsp / 15 ml   Unsalted butter

4 oz / 125 g   Onion, brunoise-cut

4 oz / 125 g   Carrot, brunoise-cut

4 oz / 125 g   Celery, brunoise-cut

3   Garlic cloves, sliced

1 tsp / 5 ml   Tomato paste

4 fl oz / 125 ml   Red wine

1 tsp / 5 ml   Rosemary, chopped fine

24 oz / 750 ml   Cannellini beans, soaked

1   Bay leaf

1 qt / 1 L   Lamb jus

1 cup / 250 ml   Panko, lightly toasted with butter

Braised Lamb

1 lb / 450 g   Lamb loin, boneless

3 tbsp / 45 ml   Olive oil

2 cups / 450 g   Braised lamb shanks, meat removed from bones, diced

as needed   Garlic chips

as needed   Fried shallot rings*

12 fl oz / 375 ml   Lamb sauce

* For fried shallot rings, dust rings lightly in flour, and deep fry for 15-20 seconds.

Method

1. In a stainless-steel bowl, combine the brown sugar and kosher salt; mix well to form a cure mixture. Add the lamb shoulder and toss to coat evenly. Cover with plastic wrap and place into the refrigerator for 12 hours.

2. Remove lamb shoulder from the refrigerator and rinse under cold running water to remove all cure mixture.

3. Pat the lamb shoulder completely dry with paper towel. Season with salt and pepper and place into a medium braising pan. Add the olive oil, smashed garlic, rosemary, and shallots.

4. Cover and place into a preheated 300°F (150°C) oven; cook until meat is tender, approximately 3–6 hours.

5. Remove the lamb shoulder from the oven and allow it to cool to room temperature. Remove the lamb shoulder from the oil and gently pull the meat into 1.5 in. (3.75 cm) pieces. Drizzle about 3 tbsp (45 ml) of the oil over the pulled shoulder meat, wrap in plastic wrap, and reserve in a warm place for service.

6. Place a medium saucepan over medium heat and add unsalted butter. When butter is almost melted, add carrots, onions, celery, and garlic.

7. Cook, stirring often, until the vegetables are tender. Add the tomato paste and continue to cook, while stirring, for 4 minutes.

8. Deglaze the saucepan with the red wine. Reduce the wine by half; add chopped rosemary, beans, bay leaf, and lamb jus. Bring to a simmer over medium heat; continue to simmer until beans are tender, approximately 1 hour.

9. Remove pan from heat and add diced lamb shank meat cassoulet. Stir to combine; season to taste with salt and pepper.

10. Divide the mixture among 6 crocks. Cover top of the mixture with toasted panko and place crocks into a preheated 325°F (160°C) oven. Bake until crumbs are golden brown. Remove from oven and reserve, warm, for service.

11. Season the lamb loin with salt and pepper.

12. Place a large heavy-bottom sauté pan over medium-high heat and add 3 tbsp (45 ml) olive oil. When the oil begins to smoke, add the loin and cook until nicely browned on all sides and desired level of doneness has been reached.

13. Remove from the pan and allow to rest for 5 minutes.

14. At time of service, be sure that all food is hot. Slice the lamb loin into the desired portion sizes and arrange on a warm buffet vessel, such as the one shown in the picture.

15. Spoon the pulled, reserved lamb confit next to the lamb loin. Ladle the lamb sauce over the lamb loin. Garnish with the fried shallots and garlic chips.

16. Serve the cassoulet separately.

Filet mignon is by far the most frequently selected menu item in the banquet world. For buffets, the challenge is to keep the filet cooked at the proper temperature. This is achieved by batch cooking at just under the desired temperature.

The short rib charlotte is a specialty item. We prepare a selection of savory charlottes for our buffet menus, as they can be made with less expensive cuts of meats, are a pleasure to eat, and hold up extremely well.

Pan-Roasted Filet Mignon of Beef with Braised Short Rib Charlottes | SERVES 6

INGREDIENTS

1–1/2 lb / 675 g	Braised short ribs, shredded
1 qt / 1 L	Short rib braising liquid
1/4 cup / 60 ml	Fig mostarda*
as needed	Kosher salt
as needed	Fresh cracked pepper
as needed	Clarified butter, melted
24 slices	White bread, crusts removed
1	Whole egg, whipped
3 tbsp / 45 ml	Olive oil
6	Filet mignons, 5 oz (150 g) each
2 tbsp / 30 ml	Unsalted butter
3 cloves	Garlic, unpeeled, smashed

2	Shallots, unpeeled, quartered
3 sprigs	Thyme
2 tbsp / 30 ml	Flat-leaf parsley, chopped
1 lb / 450 g	Vegetable of choice
1 cup / 250 ml	Red wine sauce
Red Wine Sauce	
2 tbsp / 30 ml	Butter
2	Shallots, medium, minced
1 cup / 250 ml	Dry red wine
1 cup / 250 ml	Veal stock, gelled
3 tbsp / 45 ml	Cold butter, cut into pieces
as needed	Ground black pepper and salt

Method   *Fig mostarda is a version of mustard fruits and can be purchased through a European import purveyor.*

1. Place beef short rib into a medium braising pan. Add the braising liquid and slowly warm over medium heat, 12–15 minutes. Add the fig mostarda and parsley, season to taste with kosher salt and pepper.

2. Brush six 4-oz (125-ml) ramekins well with clarified butter.

3. Using a rolling pin, roll out the bread slices to 1/8 in. (3 mm) thick. Using a round cutter the same size as the bottom of the ramekins, cut 6 circles and press 1 into each of the buttered ramekins.

4. Brush the remaining bread with the whipped egg and cut into 1-in.- (2.5-cm) thick strips.

5. Line the sides of each ramekin with the bread slices, being sure the slices overlap the tops of the ramekins.

6. Divide the short rib mixture into 6 equal portions and fill each bread-lined ramekin.

7. Fold overlapping bread slices to cover the top of the ramekins; brush well with remaining whipped egg.

8. Place the ramekins into a preheated 325°F (160°C) oven and bake until golden brown and heated through, approximately 15–20 minutes. Remove from the oven and reserve warm for service.

9. Place a heavy-bottom skillet over medium-high heat and add olive oil. Season filet mignons with salt and pepper. Once the oil begins to smoke, add filets to pan and cook for 3 minutes or until golden brown.

10. Turn filets over and add unsalted butter, garlic, shallots, and thyme. Continue to cook, while basting the meat, until filets have reached desired degree of doneness. Remove from pan and allow to rest for 5 minutes before serving.

11. To prepare red wine sauce, melt butter in a sauce pan. Add shallots and cook over low heat, stirring frequently until shallots are translucent.

12. Raise heat to high, add wine and stock, and bring to a boil, then reduce to medium simmer. Simmer liquid until reduced by half. It should be enough to coat a spoon.

13. Remove from pan from heat and whisk in butter. Season with salt and pepper.

14. At time of service, unmold the charlottes and place on the serving platter. Arrange the cooked filets next to the charlottes. Serve hot with your favorite vegetables and red wine sauce.

Skate Wing with Zucchini Envoltini and Citrus Butter Sauce | SERVES 6

INGREDIENTS

8 fl oz / 250 ml Ricotta cheese	1 Shallot, peeled and sliced
1 Egg yolk	2 sprigs Thyme
1 tbsp / 15 ml Flat-leaf parsley, chopped	1 tsp / 5 ml Heavy cream
1/2 tbsp / 7 ml Fresh basil, chopped	1/2 lb / 225 g Unsalted butter, cold, cubed
as needed Kosher salt	6 Skate wing fillets, 5 oz (150 g) each
as needed Fresh cracked pepper	1 cup / 250 ml All-purpose flour
18 Zucchini, cut into ribbons, 1/8 in. thick	3 tbsp / 45 ml Clarified butter
4 fl oz / 125 ml White wine	as needed Tomato powder
4 fl oz / 125 ml Champagne vinegar	

Method

1. In a stainless-steel bowl, combine the ricotta, egg yolk, chopped parsley, and basil. Mix well and season to taste with salt and pepper. Reserve.

2. Lay out the zucchini ribbons, 3 per serving, onto your work surface. Divide the ricotta mixture evenly between the zucchini ribbon groups. Roll the ribbons to form logs.

3. Place the logs onto a greased cookie sheet and bake in a preheated 350°F (175°C) oven until heated through, approximately 7 minutes. Remove from the oven and reserve warm for service.

4. Place the white wine, vinegar, shallots, and thyme into a small stainless-steel saucepan. Reduce to au sec over medium heat.

5. Add the heavy cream and cook for 1 minute.

6. Remove the pan from the heat and slowly whisk in the cold butter until it has melted. Strain through a fine sieve and season to taste with kosher salt. Reserve in a warm place for service. (Be careful not to allow the sauce to get too warm, or it will break.)

7. Place a large skillet over medium-high heat and preheat it for 4 minutes.

8. Season the skate wing fillets with salt and pepper and dust lightly with the flour.

9. Add the clarified butter to the hot pan and allow to melt.

Customers are less familiar with skate than with other fish species. When it is introduced, however, it tends to be well received due to its taste, texture, and moisture. Skate is also buffet-friendly; it holds well for service and is versatile. Here, the rolled zucchini adds another dimension by serving as both a very practical edible garnish for the buffet presentation and a lovely complement to the fish. And note that it follows one of the basic rules of the buffet: hot food, hot garnish.

10. Add the skate fillets and cook on one side until lightly golden. Flip the fish over and continue to cook until it is cooked through, approximately 2 minutes.

11. Remove from the pan and drain quickly on paper towels.

12. Arrange the cooked skate fillets on a service dish and place 1 warm zucchini on top of each. Drizzle the fish with the butter sauce and finish with a sprinkle of tomato powder. Serve hot.

Pan-Roasted Veal Loin, Fried Veal Cheeks, and Savory Bread Pudding | SERVES 6

It is all too easy to fall into a rut when choosing menu items to include on a buffet. One way to avoid this pitfall is to keep in mind the customer's willingness to try different food items. For example, veal is not often served on a buffet, yet we have had excellent results on a dine-around buffet when we feature veal on a station as a carved item or as a dish teamed up with flavorful accoutrements.

This buffet dish of veal loin, crispy veal cheeks, and savory bread pudding produces complementary textures and flavors too good to pass up.

INGREDIENTS

Bread Pudding

6 tbsp / 90 ml	Unsalted butter
1 tbsp / 15 ml	Onion, brunoise-cut
1 tbsp / 15 ml	Celery, brunoise-cut
1 tbsp / 15 ml	Carrot, brunoise-cut
2	Garlic cloves, sliced
1 qt / 1 L	Chicken broth
1 lb / 450 g	Brioche cubes, toasted
1 tbsp / 15 ml	Parsley, chopped
2	Whole eggs, cracked
as needed	Kosher salt
as needed	Fresh cracked pepper

Veal Cheeks

6	Veal cheeks, 3 oz (90 g) each braised and cooled
1 cup / 250 ml	All-purpose flour
3	Whole eggs, whipped
1 cup / 250 ml	Panko, ground fine

Veal Loin

6	Veal loin medallions, 4 oz (120 g) each
3 tbsp / 45 ml	Clarified butter
1 sprig	Rosemary
1 sprig	Sage
2	Garlic cloves, unpeeled, smashed
1	Shallot, unpeeled, quartered
6	Sage leaves, fried*

For fried sage leaves, select nice, whole leaves, dust lightly in flour, and deep fry for 15-20 seconds.

Method

1. To make the bread pudding, place 2 tbsp (30 ml) of unsalted butter into a medium stainless-steel saucepan and melt over low heat. Add onion, celery, carrot, and garlic and cook over low heat until vegetables are soft.

2. Add the chicken broth and bring to a boil. Remove from the heat.

3. Place the toasted brioche into a large bowl and add chopped parsley. Add hot broth and cracked eggs to the bread cubes; mix well to combine. Season to taste with salt and pepper.

4. Turn out mixture onto a large sheet of plastic wrap and roll tightly into a log. Secure ends tightly with butcher's twine. Place the log into a steamer or combi oven with steam and cook for 20 minutes, until set.

5. Remove from the steamer and allow to cool completely in the refrigerator. Remove plastic wrap and cut into 6 equal portions and reserve.

6. Place a large nonstick pan over medium-high heat and preheat for 3 minutes.

7. Add 3 tbsp (45 ml) of butter. When the butter has melted completely, add the bread pudding portions and cook on all sides until golden brown. Remove from the pan and reserve for service.

8. Dust the veal cheeks with the flour and then dip into the whipped eggs. Remove from the egg and place into the panko; toss to coat completely. Reserve.

9. Place a heavy-bottom sauté pan over medium-high heat and add clarified butter. While butter is melting, season the veal medallions. When butter begins to smoke, add the medallions to the pan. Cook on one side until golden brown.

10. Turn the medallions over and add the remaining unsalted butter along with the garlic, shallots, rosemary, and sage. Continue to cook, basting often, until the desired degree of doneness is achieved.

11. Remove from the pan and reserve warm for service.

12. Warm the bread pudding in the oven to 150°F (65°C) and place onto the service platter. Fry the veal cheeks in a preheated 350°F (175°C) fryer until golden brown. Drain on paper towels.

13. Place 1 veal cheek on top of each bread pudding portion. Arrange the hot medallions next to the veal cheeks and bread pudding. Serve with your favorite sauce and garnish with fried sage leaves. Serve hot.

Sous Vide Salmon, Morel Potato Cake, Peas, Fava Beans, and Butter Sauce | SERVES 6

INGREDIENTS

32 oz / 960 g	Mashed potatoes
2	Whole eggs, beaten
1 cup / 250 ml	All-purpose flour
2 pinches	Nutmeg, ground
1 tsp / 5 ml	Chives, snipped
16	Morels, sliced, cooked
as needed	Kosher salt
as needed	Fresh cracked pepper
1 cup / 250 ml	Potato buds
4 fl oz / 125 ml	White wine
4 fl oz / 125 ml	Champagne vinegar
1	Shallot, peeled, sliced
1 sprig	Thyme
1 tbsp / 15 ml	Heavy cream
1 lb / 450 g	Unsalted butter, cold, cubed
1	Lime, juiced
6 tbsp / 90 ml	Extra-virgin olive oil
6	Salmon mignons, 5 oz (150 g) each
4 fl oz / 125 ml	Clarified butter
1 tbsp / 15 ml	Unsalted butter
2 bunches	Ramps, cleaned
2 cups / 500 ml	Spring peas, shelled, blanched
2 cups / 500 ml	Fava beans, shelled, blanched

This buffet item, appealing to the eye, says spring has arrived! Salmon cooked in its own juices with fresh lime and olive oil, morels, peas, and fava beans join in a simple but powerful flavor marriage; it's a dish even the most discriminating buffet guest will want to try.

Method

1. In a medium mixing bowl, combine the mashed potatoes, egg, flour, nutmeg, chives, and morels. Mix well and season to taste with salt and pepper.

2. Form 6 cakes in 4-in. (10-cm) ring molds. Dredge each cake in potato buds. Reserve for service.

3. Place the white wine, vinegar, shallots, and thyme into a small stainless-steel saucepan. Over medium heat, reduce to au sec.

4. Add the heavy cream and cook for 1 minute.

5. Remove the pan from the heat and slowly whisk in the cold butter until it is all incorporated. Strain through a fine sieve. Season to taste with salt. Reserve in a warm place for service. (Do not let the sauce get too warm or it will break.)

6. Combine the lime juice and the extra-virgin olive oil.

7. Put the salmon mignons into individual Cryovac bags; divide the lime juice mixture equally among the 6 bags. Seal the bags tightly in a Cryovac machine.

8. Place the sealed bags into a 155°F (70°C) water bath for 10 minutes or until cooked through. Remove the bags from the water bath and keep warm for service.

9. At time of service, place a large nonstick pan over medium heat and add the clarified butter. Once the butter is melted, add the potato cakes and brown evenly on both sides. Be sure they are heated through. Reserve hot for service.

10. Place a large sauté pan over medium heat and add 1 tbsp (15 ml) of butter. Once the butter has melted, add the ramps and cook for 3 minutes or until tender. Add the peas and beans and cook for 2 additional minutes. Season to taste with salt and pepper.

11. Arrange an array of hot vegetables on the service platter. Remove the salmon from the bags and add to the service platter, along with the potato cakes. Drizzle the butter sauce over the fish and serve immediately.

CHAPTER SIX

FINGER FOODS

*W*hat are finger foods? Are they not just a form of canapés and hors d'oeuvre? Are they not all one in the same? The short answer is no, although the terms are often used interchangeably. The simple definition of a finger food is a small-bite item that can be picked up and eaten with one's fingers—a portion generally considered equal to one or two bites. A canapé, by contrast, is an appetizer consisting of a thin slice or piece of bread cut into shapes, buttered and toasted, or fried in butter or oil, on which savory foods are served. An hors d'oeuvre, a small savory appetizer served before a meal, customarily with cocktails, has some similarity to finger food, in that it usually is one or two bites in size and can be served cold or hot. Hors d'oeuvres may be in the form of a fancy canapé

or as simple as a selection of crudités, cheeses, and the like. The term *hors d'oeuvre* (which may be used properly for both the singular and plural forms) translates literally as "outside the work."

Finger foods are simple in preparation, big on taste, and easy to eat during a reception. And the term aside, many finger foods are accompanied by a small spoon, fork, or decorative pick so guests do not dirty their hands when enjoying the food. This, of course, raises the question of whether a finger food ceases to be one when it is served on a spoon or in another vessel and is accompanied by a salsa or salad garnish that cannot be eaten with the main item using one's fingers.

An example of a true finger food is our Peanut Butter, Jelly, and Foie Gras Sandwich (page 97), a simple yet elegant item whose rich contrast of flavors will excite the palette and yet can be eaten with the fingers in just a couple of bites. In contrast, our Olive Oil Poached Red Snapper with Cucumber Salsa (page 89) is served on a spoon, for the only way to enjoy this small treat is to use the utensil and eat the fish and salsa together. (One could argue that you use your fingers to pick up the spoon and enjoy the snapper in one bite.) An advantage of this approach is that it allows the chef greater diversity in choosing a garnish to accompany the main item.

Further stretching the definition, finger foods also can be served on individual plates for buffet presentation—as long they are on a skewer of some kind or can be picked up easily and eaten with the fingers. Plates can allow the chef to be creative in designing the edible foundations on the plate for the finger food. For example, the Smoked Jumbo Lump Crab with Crispy Cauliflower and Candied Leek (page 90) is laid on strips of candied leeks for a nice look. Feta cheese sits on an eggplant crisp, making the cheese pop; and the crisp eggplant is edible, as well.

On a buffet, combining canapés, hors d'oeuvres, and finger foods, in one form or another, offers endless possibilities and whets the customer's appetite for what's to come.

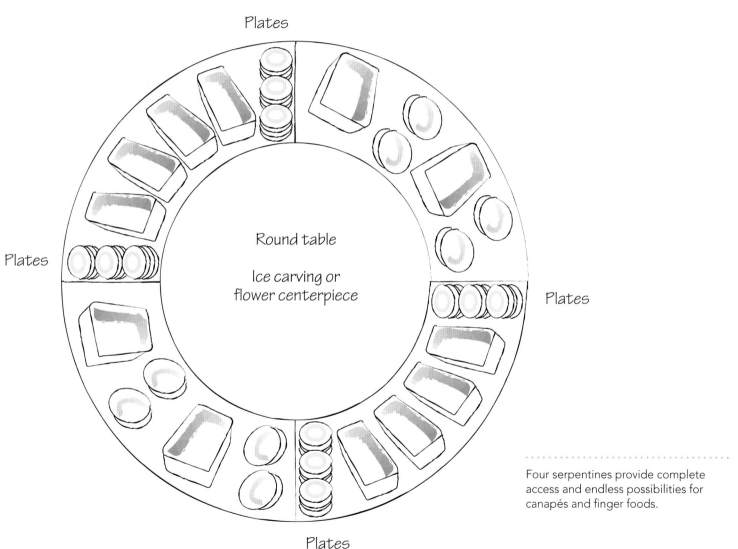

Reception Stations

Plates

Plates

Round table

Ice carving or
flower centerpiece

Plates

Plates

Plates

Four serpentines provide complete access and endless possibilities for canapés and finger foods.

Marinated Jumbo Lump Crab Club Mini Sandwich | SERVES 6

INGREDIENTS

8 oz / 225 g	Jumbo lump crabmeat
1/2	Lemon, juiced
1 tbsp / 15 ml	Extra-virgin olive oil
1 tsp / 5 ml	Flat-leaf parsley, chopped
as needed	Kosher salt
as needed	Fresh cracked black pepper

18	Brioche rounds
as needed	Butter, softened
6	Olive Oil Tomato Petals*
1 tbsp / 15 ml	Butter, softened
6	Quail eggs

*Refer to Appendix A, "From the Chef's Pantry" (p. 202), for this signature recipe.

Method

1. Place the crabmeat into a stainless-steel bowl and add the lemon juice, extra-virgin olive oil, and parsley. Season to taste with salt and pepper and then toss lightly to combine. Cover with plastic and place into the refrigerator until time of service.

2. Lightly rub both sides of the brioche rounds with the butter. Preheat a large sauté pan over medium heat for 3 minutes. Place the buttered brioche rounds into the pan and brown lightly on both sides. Remove from the pan and reserve for service at room temperature.

3. Place 6 toasted brioche rounds onto work surface and divide marinated crabmeat evenly among them. Lay a toasted brioche round on top of the marinated crabmeat.

4. Place one tomato petal on top of second brioche round and top petal with a third toasted brioche round.

5. Place a medium nonstick sauté pan over medium heat and add 1 tbsp (15 ml) of butter. When the butter begins to bubble, gently crack the quail eggs into the pan. Cook the eggs to the desired doneness.

6. Remove the eggs from the pan and place onto a cutting board. Using a ring cutter, trim the eggs to the same size as the toasted brioche rounds.

7. Lay one trimmed egg on top of each of the sandwiches; insert a toothpick to secure the sandwich. Serve immediately at room temperature.

When you offer something new, combine it with something familiar and you will increase the chances of its success. This recipe is a good example. Customers are, of course, familiar with the club sandwich; it has long been a favorite on menus in establishments large and small. I create many versions of this sandwich; this crab club is just one. Try your own variations for more diverse buffet choices; just remember, keep the concept simple and combine flavors that are naturally harmonious.

Olive Oil Poached Red Snapper with Cucumber Salsa | **SERVES 6**

INGREDIENTS

16 fl oz / 500 ml	Extra-virgin olive oil
2 sprigs	Thyme
1 sprig	Rosemary
1	Shallot, sliced
1	Garlic clove, smashed
3 tbsp / 45 ml	Cucumber, brunoise-cut
1 tsp / 5 ml	Red bell pepper, brunoise-cut

1 tsp / 5 ml	Yellow bell pepper, brunoise-cut
1 tsp / 5 ml	Red onion, brunoise-cut
1/2 tsp / 2 ml	Champagne vinegar
1 tbsp / 15 ml	Extra-virgin olive oil
as needed	Kosher salt
as needed	Fresh cracked black pepper
6 portions	Red snapper, 1–1/2 oz (45 g) each

Method

1. Place the extra-virgin olive oil, thyme, rosemary, shallots, and garlic into a medium stainless-steel saucepan.

2. Place the pan over medium-low heat. Bring to 160°F (70°C). Allow the herbs, garlic, and shallots to infuse the oil for 10 minutes.

3. In a small stainless-steel bowl, combine the cucumber, red and yellow bell pepper, onion, vinegar, and 1 tbsp (15 ml) of extra-virgin olive oil. Season to taste with salt and pepper and then toss lightly to combine. Reserve at room temperature for service.

4. Season the red snapper portions lightly with salt and pepper. Place the fish in the 160°F (70°C) oil, and poach until cooked through, approximately 7 minutes.

5. Arrange 6 service vessels on your work surface and divide the salsa evenly among the vessels.

6. Remove the poached red snapper from the oil and drain lightly on paper towels. Season the fish lightly with kosher salt. Lay 1 portion of snapper on each of the service vessels, and serve immediately.

Poaching as a way to cook fish has been popular for many years. The traditional way to poach is in a court bouillon; here, the bouillon is replaced by olive oil. The results are stellar, creating a moist, flavorful fish that holds well for buffet service and has a flavor dimension that many customers have never experienced, but will enjoy. The only rule is, stay away from fattier fishes, such as salmon or mackerel, when poaching with oil.

Smoking adds another flavor profile to simple foods that are rich with flavor on their own. The key to finger foods or small-plate items is to ensure that they are big on flavor. In this recipe, the smoked crab is complemented by the sweet leek and crisp cauliflower.

Smoked Jumbo Lump Crab with Crispy Cauliflower and Candied Leek | SERVES 6

INGREDIENTS

1 Leek, cleaned	3 Eggs, whipped
3 cups / 700 ml Simple Syrup*	1 cup / 250 ml Fine panko
6 Cauliflower florets, small	6 Smoked jumbo lump crabmeat sections
1/2 cup / 125 ml All-purpose flour	as needed Vanilla sea salt

Refer to Appendix A, "From the Chef's Pantry" (p. 204) for this signature recipe.

Method

1. Bring 1 quart (1 L) of water to rolling boil. Add leek greens and cook 30 seconds. Remove and cool completely.

2. Using your fingers, split the leek greens in half lengthwise.

3. Bring simple syrup to a simmer and remove from heat. Add split leek greens and allow to sit 1 minute.

4. Remove leek greens and lay them onto a sheet pan lined with Silpat®. Place into a 200°F (95°C) oven for approximately 1 hour, to dry. Once dry, remove from the oven; reserve for service.

5. Put cauliflower florets in the flour and toss to coat. Shake off excess flour and add cauliflower to whipped eggs.

6. Remove the florets from the eggs and add to the panko, coating evenly. Reserve for service.

7. At time of service, arrange 6 service vessels on work surface. Using a sharp knife, cut 6 equal squares from the candied leek and arrange on service vessels.

8. Place one piece of the smoked crab onto each square of candied leek.

9. Place breaded cauliflower into a preheated 350°F (175°C) deep fryer and cook until golden brown. Remove from the fryer; drain on paper towels.

10. Place one piece of fried cauliflower onto each portion of smoked crab and secure with a toothpick.

11. Lightly sprinkle each plate with vanilla sea salt and serve immediately.

Seared Atlantic Salmon with Shaved Asparagus I SERVES 6

INGREDIENTS

3	Jumbo asparagus
1/2	Lemon, juiced
as needed	Extra-virgin olive oil
as needed	Sea salt
as needed	Fresh cracked pepper
6	Salmon mignons, 1–1/2 oz (45 g) each

Another key to successful finger foods is to make them relatively simplistic in nature. The art of achieving this is to offset textures with flavors. This salmon recipe does just that. The seared fish has a buttery profile that is balanced by asparagus, which is marinated in lemon and olive oil.

Method

1. Using a mandoline, slice the asparagus lengthwise into thin strips. Reserve any scraps for later use.

2. Place the asparagus strips into a stainless-steel bowl and toss with lemon juice, extra-virgin olive oil, salt, and pepper. Reserve for service.

3. Preheat a heavy-bottom sauté pan over medium-high heat for 3 minutes.

4. Lightly season the salmon with salt, pepper, and olive oil.

5. Place the salmon into the hot pan and sear on one side for 2–3 minutes, until it is almost cooked. Remove from the pan and reserve in a warm place while you prepare the service plates.

6. Arrange 6 service plates on your work surface and lay 1 ribbon of asparagus on each plate.

7. Wrap each piece of salmon in an asparagus ribbon and place it onto the service plate. Lightly drizzle with extra-virgin olive oil, and serve.

Marinated Feta Cheese with Eggplant and Olives | SERVES 6

INGREDIENTS

6	Feta cheese cubes, 1/2 in. (1 cm)
1 tsp / 5 ml	Fresh oregano, chopped
1/2 tsp / 2 ml	Fresh parsley, chopped
1/2 tsp / 2 ml	Fresh basil, chopped
as needed	Extra-virgin olive oil
as needed	Kosher salt
as needed	Fresh cracked pepper
6	Kalamata olives
1	Eggplant

Method

1. Place the cubes of feta cheese into a stainless-steel bowl. Add the oregano, parsley, and basil. Season lightly with extra-virgin olive oil, salt, and pepper. Toss lightly to coat. Reserve for service.

2. Using a knife, cut the eggplant into 6 very thin slices, lengthwise. Trim them to fit your service plate.

3. Lay one slice on each service plate. Lightly drizzle with extra-virgin olive oil and season lightly with salt and pepper.

4. Set one cube of the marinated feta cheese onto each of the eggplant slices.

5. Place an olive on top of each feta cube and secure with a toothpick.

6. Serve at room temperature.

The flavors of the Mediterranean influence many dishes that customers enjoy. The key to this simple finger food is the feta cheese. Strictly speaking, "real" feta is produced exclusively in Greece; it is considered a traditional Greek cheese par excellence. Soft feta, in contrast, is sweeter and more mild than its hard counterpart, which is saltier and more pronounced in flavor.

Strawberries with Avocado and Basil | SERVES 6

INGREDIENTS

6	Strawberries
1	Avocado, ripe
1	Lime, juiced
1 tsp / 5 ml	Fresh basil, chopped
as needed	Kosher salt
6	Brioche rounds, toasted

Method

1. Using a knife, remove the top from the strawberries and discard.

2. Using a small Parisienne scoop, extract the center of each strawberry and reserve.

3. Cut the avocado in half; remove the pit and outer skin.

4. Place into a stainless-steel bowl, add the lime juice and basil, and mash lightly with a fork. Season to taste with kosher salt.

5. Using a small spoon, fill the center of each strawberry with the avocado mixture. Reserve the remaining mixture for other uses.

6. Lay out the toasted brioche rounds onto plates or a platter

7. Set one strawberry, point side up, onto each brioche round.

8. Place one reserved strawberry center on top of each strawberry and secure with a toothpick. Serve at room temperature.

Two unique flavors that go really well together are strawberry and avocado. The sweet and tart of the berries are a delectable match to the creaminess of the avocado; and basil is the herb that brings them together in a small finger food that is refreshing and presents well.

Prosciutto, Oven-Dried Tomatoes, and Ratatouille on Crostini | SERVES 6

INGREDIENTS

6 Grape tomatoes, peeled	1 tbsp / 15 ml Zucchini, brunoise-cut
as needed Kosher salt	1 tbsp / 15 ml Yellow squash, brunoise-cut
as needed Fresh cracked pepper	1 tbsp / 15 ml Eggplant, brunoise-cut
as needed Extra-virgin olive oil	1 tbsp / 15 ml Tomato, brunoise-cut
1/2 Garlic clove, minced	1/4 tsp / 1 ml Fresh thyme, chopped
1 tsp / 5 ml Onion, minced	6 slices Proscuitto de Parma
1 tbsp / 15 ml Red bell pepper, brunoise-cut	6 Crostini

Method

1. Place the peeled grape tomatoes into a stainless-steel bowl and toss with extra-virgin olive oil, kosher salt, and pepper.

2. Place the tomatoes onto a pan with a roasting rack and put in a preheated 275°F (135°C) oven. Roast for 15 minutes.

3. Remove from the oven and allow to cool to room temperature.

4. Place a small sauté pan over medium heat and add 1 tbsp (15 ml) of extra-virgin olive oil.

5. Add the garlic and onions and cook until garlic is soft and onion is translucent.

6. Add the red pepper and cook for 3 minutes. Add the zucchini, yellow squash, and eggplant and cook for an additional 2 minutes.

7. Add the tomato and thyme and cook for 2 more minutes. Remove the pan from the heat and season the ratatouille to taste with salt and pepper. Allow to cool to room temperature.

8. Roll the prosciutto and lay a slice on each piece of crostini.

9. Add a roasted tomato to each of the crostini, along with a portion of the ratatouille. Serve at room temperature.

Here, the flavors of the Mediterranean meet on a crostini. The saltiness of the prosciutto, sweetness of the tomatoes, and the spice of the vegetables add up to big flavor on an olive oil crostini.

Tomato and Mozzarella Skewer with Roasted Zucchini and Basil Oil | **SERVES 6**

Another favorite, tomato and mozzarella, is teamed up in this recipe with roasted zucchini, and complemented by basil oil, in a one- or two-bite item that presents well on a buffet and evokes customer comfort.

INGREDIENTS

6 slices	Zucchini, 1/2 in. (1 cm)	6	Cherry tomatoes
as needed	Extra-virgin olive oil	as needed	Basil oil
as needed	Kosher salt	6 slices	Fresh mozzarella, 1/4 in. (1/2 cm)
as needed	Fresh cracked pepper	6	Picholine olives, pitted

Method

1. Place zucchini slices into stainless-steel bowl; toss lightly with extra-virgin olive oil. Season to taste with salt and pepper.

2. Place seasoned zucchini onto roasting pan with a rack and into a preheated 350°F (175°C) oven.

3. Roast zucchini until it begins to brown and becomes tender, approximately 7 minutes. Remove from oven and cool to room temperature.

4. Cut tomatoes in half and place into a stainless-steel bowl. Toss lightly with basil oil. Season with salt and pepper. Reserve at room temperature.

5. Using a fluted ring cutter, cut mozzarella slices to same size as cherry tomatoes. Add cheese to seasoned tomatoes; toss lightly.

6. At time of service, arrange 6 service plates on work surface.

7. Using a knife, cut a section off roasted zucchini slices so they will stand on their side on service plates.

8. With a knife, make a small groove in top of each zucchini slice to hold tomato and mozzarella skewer.

9. Insert half a tomato on a bamboo skewer. Add a piece of mozzarella and the other tomato half to the skewer. Repeat with all tomatoes and mozzarella. Top each skewer with an olive.

10. Rest each skewer on a roasted zucchini slice across a service plate.

11. Finish with a drizzle of basil oil. Serve at room temperature.

Peanut Butter, Jelly, and Foie Gras Club Sandwich | SERVES 6

INGREDIENTS

18	Brioche rounds
as needed	Soft butter
3 oz / 85 g	Foie Gras Torchon*
6 tsp / 90 g	Organic peanut butter
6 tsp / 90 g	Quality strawberry or grape preserves

*Refer to Appendix A, "From the Chef's Pantry" (p. 197), for this signature recipe.

Method

1. Preheat a large nonstick sauté pan over medium heat for 2 minutes.

2. Rub each side of the brioche rounds with soft butter and place into the preheated pan. Cook until lightly golden brown on both sides. Remove from the pan and lay onto your work surface.

3. Place a portion of foie gras torchon onto 6 of the toasted brioche rounds.

4. Spread 1 tsp (5 ml) of peanut butter on the 6 toasted brioche rounds. Place 1 round on top of each foie gras round, peanut butter side up.

5. Top each sandwich with a final toasted brioche round.

6. Dollop 1 tsp (5 ml) of the jelly on top of each sandwich; secure the sandwich with a toothpick. Serve at room temperature.

Now here's a club sandwich that's both decadent and fun. This foie gras club sandwich is accompanied by creamy peanut butter and sweet jelly and served on a buttery brioche.

Try a variety of petite club sandwiches on your buffet. They are fun and simple to prepare, hold well, and are real treats for the customer. Remember, customers are much more likely to try new items from a buffet than they are from an à la carte menu.

CHAPTER SEVEN

FROM THE GLASS

When designing modern buffet presentations, no matter how creative, it is essential to stay focused on the number-one objective of any buffet, which is to offer the guests variety, allowing them to choose, taste, and sample.

Glass lends itself to the display of fresh vibrant colors, textures, and consumable garnishes to complement the dishes on your buffet. It is a clean, elegant material for enhancing creative and refreshing small-bite foods, whether richly or lightly seasoned. And by adding little touches of flavored oils, syrups, and vinegars you can both highlight the presentation and add a finishing piquancy to your creations.

Today's chefs can purchase glasses in all shapes and sizes to use for receptions, pastry displays, and even dinners, from savory stations that place a meal such as roast turkey in a martini glass to soup shooters in small glasses, described in Chapter 11.

The advantage to using glass as a serving vessel that it provides a clear view of both the flavors and textures the chef has chosen for a special food item. Glass also makes it possible to serve fresh waters, such as tomato water and strawberry water, as shooters, for a refreshing treat. Garnished with a pick of marinated foods that are eaten before or after guests drink the water—depending on the concept of the shooter—will add complexity and elegance that excites the taste buds. Take, for example, the Prosciutto and Melon Shooter (p. 101). The salted, cured ham is complemented by the natural sweetness of the small melon balls. Then, a chaser of fresh melon water can be infused with herbs, if desired, and honey and other flavoring items.

Buffet Zone for Smaller Spaces

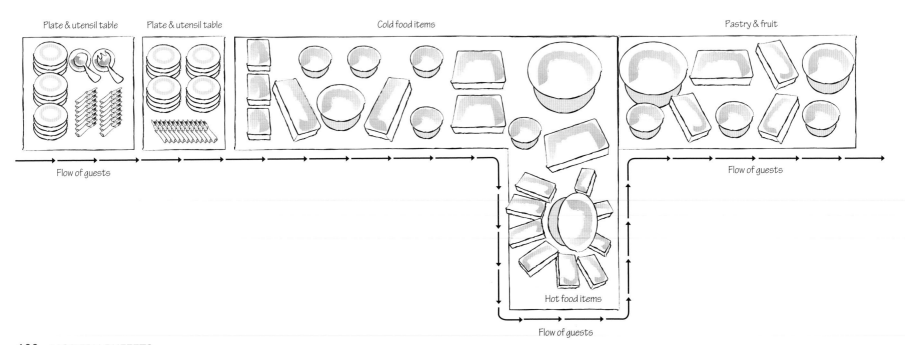

Plate & utensil table Plate & utensil table Cold food items Pastry & fruit

Flow of guests

Flow of guests

Hot food items

Flow of guests

Prosciutto and Melon Shooter | SERVES 8

INGREDIENTS

2   Honeydew melons, ripe

1   Crenshaw melon, ripe

8 fl oz / 250 ml   Simple Syrup*

8 slices   Proscuitto or Serrano ham

8   Bamboo toothpicks or other skewers or picks

Refer to Appendix A, "From the Chef's Pantry" (p. 204), for this signature recipe.

Method

1. Cut both melons in half and remove the seeds from their centers.

2. Using a Parisienne scoop, form 8 balls from each melon and reserve.

3. Remove the outer skin from the melons and cut them into 1-in. (2.5-cm) pieces.

4. Place all the melon pieces into a food processor, along with half of the simple syrup. Process on high for 2 minutes.

5. Line a stainless-steel bowl with 3 layers of cheesecloth; pour the puréed melon into the cheesecloth. Using butcher's twine, tie the cheesecloth closed, leaving a length of twine for hanging the bundle.

6. Put the bowl into the refrigerator and hang the cheesecloth bundle so it extends at least 6 in. (15 cm) above the bottom of the bowl. Leave it in the refrigerator overnight to collect the liquid.

7. The next day, remove the bowl from the refrigerator and discard the cheesecloth. Taste the liquid and adjust with the simple syrup if needed.

8. Divide the liquid equally between 8 glasses.

9. Insert 1 ball of honeydew melon on a toothpick or skewer, followed by a folded slice of ham. Complete each skewer with a ball of Crenshaw melon.

10. Lay the skewer across the top of each glass and serve.

The advantage to this shooter is name recognition. Prosciutto and melon is a well-known combination and a guest favorite. The secret of its success derives from the balance of sweet, salty, and refreshing flavors that make it so delectable.

For additional flavor profiles with this recipe, steep the simple syrup with spices such as clove or star anise.

Ceviche is seafood that has been marinated and "cold-cooked," so to speak, by the acid in the marinade. Easy to prepare and full of flavor, this shellfish dish is a recognizable favorite for the guest.

Ceviche Shooter | SERVES 8

INGREDIENTS

8 oz / 240 g   Fresh sea scallops, diced

8 oz / 240 g   Fresh shrimp, peeled, deveined, chopped

6   Limes, juiced

1 tsp / 5 ml   Kosher salt

1 tbsp / 15 ml   Tomato, peeled, finely diced

1 tbsp / 15 ml   Red onion, finely diced

2 tbsp / 30 ml   Cucumber, finely diced

1 oz / 30 g   Micro greens

1 fl oz / 30 ml   Extra-virgin olive oil

Method

1. Place the scallops and shrimp into a stainless-steel mixing bowl. Add the lime juice and salt and mix thoroughly. Cover with plastic wrap and put into the refrigerator for 4 hours.

2. Upon removal from the refrigerator, add the tomato, onion, and cucumber and mix thoroughly. Cover with plastic wrap and put back into the refrigerator for an additional 2 hours.

3. Taste the ceviche and adjust the seasoning, if needed, with salt.

4. Divide the ceviche and its juices evenly between 8 glasses.

5. Toss the micro greens lightly in extra-virgin olive oil and place a small amount on top of the ceviche in the glasses. Serve well chilled.

Lobster Grapefruit Shooter | SERVES 8

INGREDIENTS

4	Grapefruits, juiced
1 tsp / 5 ml	Clover honey
2 fl oz / 60 ml	Quality champagne
8 oz / 240 g	Lobster knuckle meat, cooked
1	Lime
8	Flat-leaf parsley leaves
8	Bamboo toothpicks or other skewers or picks

Method

1. In a stainless-steel mixing bowl, combine the fresh grapefruit juice, honey, and champagne; mix until the honey dissolves. Chill thoroughly.

2. While the mixture is chilling, stick 1 oz (30 g) of lobster knuckle meat on a bamboo skewer or toothpick. Wrap tightly in plastic wrap, forming a tube shape. Place into the refrigerator until time of service.

3. At time of service, evenly divide the chilled grapefruit mixture between 8 glasses.

4. Cut the lime into 8 slices and garnish each glass.

5. Remove the plastic from the lobster skewers and lay one skewer across the top of each glass. Finish each shooter with a piece of flat-leaf parsley.

Who doesn't enjoy lobster? Here, the sweetness of the knuckle meat is complemented by the bubbly citrus flavor of grapefruit. To make it even more special, add little pearls of caviar to the shooter.

Savory Strawberry Shooter | SERVES 8

INGREDIENTS

4 pt / 1.8 kg Strawberries, overripe, stems removed

2 tbsp / 30 ml Sugar

2 Limes, juiced

1 tbsp / 15 ml Clover honey

5 sprigs Fresh basil

pinch Kosher salt

8 Blackberries

8 Strawberry chips, dried

8 Bamboo toothpicks or other skewers or picks

Fresh strawberries are full of flavor, and when you combine their rich sweetness with basil and a splash of lime, you have a refreshing shooter that the guest will want to drink as a full glass. The best way to serve this shooter is to chill the juice at 38°F (3°C).

Method

1. Place the strawberries, sugar, lime juice, honey, basil, and salt into a food processor; blend on high speed for 2 minutes.

2. Line a medium bowl with 3 layers of cheesecloth. Pour the puréed mixture into the cheesecloth. Fold the cheesecloth up and tie tightly with butcher's twine, leaving a length to hang the cheesecloth bundle.

3. Put the bowl into the refrigerator and tie the cheesecloth so that it hangs at least 6 in. (15 cm) from the bottom of the bowl. Allow the purée to hang for at least 24 hours over the bowl to collect the liquid.

4. Remove the bowl from the refrigerator and discard the cheesecloth. Taste the strawberry water and adjust the taste, as needed, with more honey and lime juice.

5. Divide the seasoned strawberry water between 8 small glasses. Garnish each glass with a skewered blackberry and dried strawberry chip. (Another option is a skewer of raspberries drizzled with cocoa sauce.)

Savory Raspberry Shooter | SERVES 8

INGREDIENTS

3 pt / 1.3 kg   Raspberries

3 sprigs   Sage

8 fl oz / 250 ml   Simple Syrup*

16 pieces   Dried raspberries

2 oz / 60 ml   Crème fraîche

Refer to Appendix A, "From the Chef's Pantry" (p. 204), for this signature recipe.

Method

1. Place the raspberries, sage, and simple syrup into a blender; process on high for 2 minutes.

2. Strain the liquid through a fine sieve and chill thoroughly.

3. Divide the liquid evenly between 8 glasses.

4. Garnish each glass with a dollop of crème fraîche and a few dried raspberries.

Raspberries, with their tart and sweet flavor profile, make a great juice; the sage in this recipe adds a complexity that energizes the taste buds. The richness of the crème fraîche is a fine finish. For a little more pick-me-up, add a splash of sparkling water or champagne to the shooters.

Mangoes produce a juice that is something special, one with body. In this recipe, it is accented by the lime and the crunchy sweetness of the meringue, and finished with the sweet spice of micro greens.

Mango Shooter | SERVES 8

INGREDIENTS

2   Ripe mangoes, peeled, pit removed, and diced

6   Navel oranges, juiced

2 tbsp / 30 ml   Lime juice, fresh

2 tbsp / 30 ml   Clover honey

8   Mini meringue cookies

1 oz / 30 g   Basil micro greens

1 tsp / 5 ml   Almond oil

Method

1. Place the mango, orange juice, lime juice, and honey into a blender; process on high for 2 minutes.

2. Strain the liquid through a fine sieve and chill thoroughly.

3. Divide the liquid evenly between 8 glasses.

4. Place a mini meringue cookie into each glass.

5. Toss the micro greens lightly in the almond oil and arrange a small amount on top of each shooter.

Foie Gras Mousse
with Cranberry Compote | SERVES 6

Foie gras is the finest example of simplicity combined with elegance. Prepared here as a light mousse with the cranberry compote, the result is a winning balance of sweet, fatty, smooth, and tart. To make it seasonal, you can substitute rhubarb or berries or even fig compote.

INGREDIENTS

1/2 lb / 225 g	Fresh cranberries
1 tbsp / 15 ml	Orange zest, grated
1 tsp / 5 ml	Lemon zest, grated
1/2 cup / 125 ml	Orange juice, fresh
3 tbsp / 45 ml	Lemon juice, fresh
1/2 cup / 125 ml	Sugar
1 tsp / 5 ml	Vanilla extract
10 fl oz / 310 ml	Water

3 tbsp / 45 ml	Cornstarch
1 lobe	Grade A foie gras, cleaned and trimmed, at room temperature
2 fl oz / 60 ml	Cognac
3 fl oz / 90 ml	Heavy cream
as needed	Kosher salt
as needed	Black pepper, freshly ground

Method

1. Put cranberries, orange and lemon zest, orange and lemon juice, sugar, vanilla, and 8 fl oz (250 ml) of water in a medium nonreactive saucepan over medium-high heat. Bring to a boil and cook 8 minutes.

2. Dissolve cornstarch in remaining water and add to pan; whisk well.
   Reduce heat to medium; whisk constantly until mixture thickens, about 2 minutes.

3. Remove from heat and cool completely.

4. Dice foie gras and marinate with brandy; let sit in the refrigerator for 30 minutes.

5. In a food processor fitted with a metal blade, add the foie gras and purée until smooth.
   Add the cream slowly; process until smooth. Season with salt and pepper.

6. Remove the mousse from the processor and spoon into 6 service vessels.

7. Top the foie gras with a spoonful of cranberry compote. Serve chilled.

CHAPTER EIGHT

SMALL PLATES, BIG FLAVORS

Small plates are new to buffet service and can be a welcome addition to a reception or dinner buffet. Old-style buffets featured all food on platters, mirrors, and other service vessels. Many of the accoutrements to the main items were available off to the side. Whether it was a sauce, chutney, or vinaigrette, the food was presented plainly, prelayered on the platter, with the flavoring components displayed separately. In the case of salad-type items, bowls were used and the dressing was tossed with the components in advance.

In the à la carte kitchen, the *amuse-bouche* (French for "amuse the mouth"), a small tasting of food, is prepared to offer guests, typically while they are waiting for their first course, compliments of the chef, as a way to showcase the chef's cooking style and to whet their appetite for the meal to come.

TEMPTING THE GUEST

Small plates of about 2 to 3 inches (3 to 8 cm), or even an espresso cup or a small glass, are used to present these tasty treats. This concept has recently caught on in the buffet sector, as a way to offer more creative foods that are, in a sense, complete appetizers. In preparing these small plates chefs can also introduce many flavor profiles to enhance the food, from infused oils to powders to nut dust, dried vegetables, and more. It's important to point out, however, that these are often items that would *not* work on a platter. Even if placed on the side of a platter, the customer might *not* be willing to try these foods, especially if they do not know what they are.

The small-plate approach also makes it easier to keep buffet selections fresh. Plates can be prepprepped and then finished with all their accoutrements just before the plates go onto the buffet. Small-plate preparation is a component process: You build the plates as you go. The advantages to this process are, one, items not put together on the plates can be fully used for the next party, or even as an amuse-bouche for the restaurant; two, you can make use of leftover products from other functions, thereby saving on food costs. For example, seared tuna loin left from a lunch party can be sliced and placed on a variety of items, from pickled cucumbers with wasabi dressing to candied ginger slaw. Leftover wild mushrooms from a banquet can be pressed into a terrine mold, sliced, and then drizzled with a tarragon mayonnaise. Your knowledge of food and flavor combinations will enable you to create a small-plate menu that is always changing and pleasing your guests.

On the buffet table, small-plate foods should be presented as grab-and-go items, so that people at, say, a reception can sample and taste many items in an elegant manner, rather than piling large amounts of several types of food on a single plate. Small plates should hold items that can be eaten in two to three bites, at most. These plates should be garnished simply and, more importantly, with edible garnishes that add flavor to the main item at hand. Take our Butter-Poached Pears, Compressed Blue Cheese, and Almonds (page 115). The garnish, composed of almonds and extra-virgin olive oil, is a natural match for the sweetened pears and sharp blue-veined cheese.

Small plates on a buffet also should be simple in nature—three to four flavor profiles and foods that the customer can recognize. On most reception-style buffets, especially the modern ones, very little signage is used. That means, however, that it's essential to assign service staff to watch over the buffet, so that they can answer any questions the guests may have—the most common being, of course, "What is that?" Covering items, or masking them will only put off customers, making them less likely to try the dishes. For items such as parfaits, panna cotta, or puréed selections, it can be helpful to display small but simple cards to identify them. An alternative is to feature a small but complete menu of the buffet offerings, so that guests can easily identify the small plates and other items.

By incorporating flavors that marry well, focusing on a variety of textures, and using fresh ingredients, the possibilities for small plates are endless, as you'll see in this selection of recipes and their presentations.

Large Double-Sided Buffet

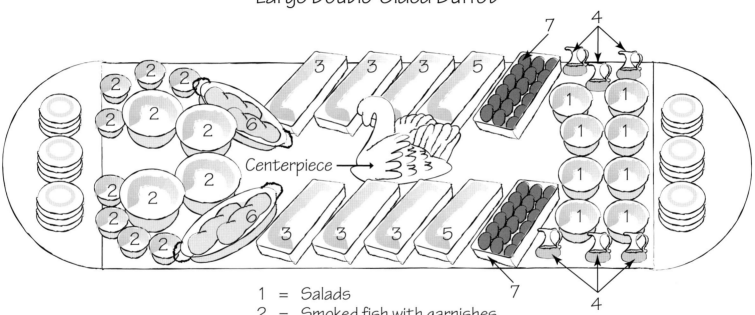

Centerpiece →

1 = Salads
2 = Smoked fish with garnishes
3 = Main plate items
4 = Dressing
5 = Cheese display
6 = Bread & butter display
7 = Sliced meat display

White Peach Panna Cotta, Pressed Fruit, Dried Raspberries, and Aged Balsamic Syrup | SERVES 10

Panna cotta is usually an item from the pastry kitchen. In this version, it becomes a savory small plate that is perfect for buffet receptions. The creaminess of the panna cotta combined with pressed fruit, the texture of dried raspberries, and balsamic vinegar make for a refreshing small plate selection.

INGREDIENTS

1 cup / 225 g Seedless watermelon, peeled	1/2 cup / 115 g Sugar
1 cup / 225 g Cantaloupe, peeled	as needed Kosher salt
1 cup / 225 g Honeydew melon, peeled	4 tbsp / 60 ml White peach purée
2 tbsp / 30 ml Powdered gelatin	1–1/2 tsp / 20 ml Vanilla extract
1/4 cup / 60 ml Simple Syrup*	1/2 cup / 125 ml Sour cream
1–1/2 tsp / 8 ml Powdered gelatin	2 tbsp / 30 ml Dried raspberries, crushed
2 tbsp / 30 ml White peach juice, cold	as needed Balsamic syrup
2–1/2 cups / 565 ml Heavy cream	10 sprigs Micro basil

Refer to Appendix A, "From the Chef's Pantry" (p. 204), for this signature recipe.

Method

1. Using a sharp knife, slice all of the melon 1/8 in. (3 mm) thick and place into a stainless-steel mixing bowl.

2. Add the powdered gelatin to the simple syrup and allow to sit for 5 minutes.

3. Gently heat the simple syrup just enough to melt the gelatin.

4. Add the simple syrup to the sliced fruit and toss to coat evenly.

5. Place all of the sliced fruit into a medium Cryovac® bag and seal tightly.

6. With a rolling pin, and using a little pressure, spread the fruit so that it is evenly pressed, approximately 1/2 in. (1 cm) thick.

7. Place the fruit, flat, into the refrigerator for at least 2 hours.

8. To make the panna cotta, sprinkle the 1–1/2 tsp (8 ml) of powdered gelatin over the peach juice and allow to sit for 5 minutes.

9. In a small stainless-steel saucepan, warm the cream with the sugar, pinch of salt, peach purée, and vanilla. Do not let it boil; warm it just enough to melt the sugar completely.

10. Add the gelatin and white peach juice to the warm cream and stir to dissolve the gelatin.

11. In a stainless-steel bowl, gently whisk together the sour cream and the warm cream, adding a little at a time, until smooth.

12. Prepare 10 small cylinder molds by lining them with acetate. Place the molds onto a flat pan and fill them gently with the panna cotta cream mixture.

13. Place on an even surface in the refrigerator and chill for at least 2 hours.

14. At time of service, remove the pressed fruit from the refrigerator and cut into small planks of about 1/2 in. × 2 in. (1 cm × 5 cm). Place 1 plank onto each service plate.

15. Unmold the panna cotta and place 1 each on the fruit planks.

16. Finish each with a sprinkle of crushed dried raspberries, a drizzle of balsamic syrup, and a sprig of micro basil. Serve chilled.

Beet Spheres and Goat Cheese with Balsamic Syrup | SERVES 10

INGREDIENTS

3 Red beets*, large	1 sprig Thyme
1 qt / 1 L Apple juice	as needed Extra-virgin olive oil
3 tbsp / 45 g Powdered gelatin	as needed Balsamic syrup
1 lb / 450 g Goat cheese	as needed Red sea salt
4 oz / 125 g Micro arugula	1 tsp / 5 ml Thyme sprigs

*If you have beets on your menu, using up the beet scraps or ends from cutting and trimming is an ideal alternative to the 3 whole beets called for here. About 3 cups would work.

Beets and goat cheese are a natural combination. This modern presentation merges wonderful flavors and seasoning in a truly memorable small plate.

Method

1. Place beets, unpeeled, into a medium stainless-steel saucepan. Add apple juice and bring to a simmer over medium-high heat. Continue to simmer beets until they are very tender, approximately 15–20 minutes.

2. Once the beets are tender, remove from the liquid and allow to cool enough for handling. Remove 1/4 cup (60 ml) of the liquid and cool completely. Reserve the remaining liquid at room temperature.

3. Once the beets have cooled, remove their skins, and dice.

4. Add the diced beets to a food processor and purée on high, until smooth. You may need to use some of the reserved warm cooking liquid for this step, but be careful to use only enough to purée the beets.

5. Pour the purée into a stainless-steel bowl and cool.

6. Sprinkle the powdered gelatin into the cooled cooking liquid and allow to sit for 5 minutes.

7. Heat the liquid just enough to melt the gelatin. Add it to the purée and mix well. Pour the beet mixture into prepared sphere molds and place them into the refrigerator to set for at least 2 hours.

8. Place the goat cheese into a Cryovac bag and seal tightly. Using a rolling pin, gently press the cheese to an even thickness, about 1/4 in. (6 mm). Place the cheese into the refrigerator to chill for 1 hour.

9. At time of service, remove the goat cheese from the refrigerator and cut into 10 small planks. Lay 1 plank at the center of each service plate. Reserve any remaining cheese for later use.

10. Unmold the beet spheres and place 1 on the top of one end of each of the cheese planks. Arrange a small amount of arugula opposite the beet sphere on the cheese plank.

11. Dress each plate with a drizzle of extra-virgin olive oil and aged balsamic vinegar. Finish by topping each beet sphere with red sea salt and some thyme. Serve at room temperature.

Butter-Poached Pears, Compressed Blue Cheese, and Almonds | SERVES 10

INGREDIENTS

2 lb / 900 g	Unsalted butter
4	Suckle pears, peeled
1/2 lb / 225 g	Blue cheese
8 oz / 225 g	Sliced almonds, toasted
as needed	Extra-virgin olive oil

Method

1. Place the butter into a stainless-steel saucepan and begin to melt over medium heat.

2. Once butter is almost completely melted, turn heat to high and cook until milk solids begin to brown.

3. Add the peeled pears and lower the heat to medium.

4. Simmer the pears in the butter until tender; remove them from the butter and allow them to cool to room temperature. Reserve the browned butter for later use.

5. Place the blue cheese into a medium Cryovac bag and seal tightly.

6. Using a rolling pin, press the cheese until it is 1/4 in. (6 mm) thick. Place the cheese into the refrigerator for at least 1 hour, to firm it up.

7. In a food processor, chop fine 3/4 cup (175 ml) of the almonds; reserve for service.

8. After the pears have cooled, cut them into 6 equal-size wedges. Using a small round cutter, remove the core from the center of each wedge.

9. Take the blue cheese from the refrigerator. With the same round cutter used on the pears, cut 10 rounds from the pressed cheese.

10. Place 1 round of cheese onto each of the 10 serving plates.

11. Arrange 2 wedges of poached pears on each plate, 1 on either side of the blue cheese round.

12. With the chopped almonds, form a line on each of the plates, next to the cheese and pears.

13. Lay a few slices of the unchopped toasted almonds on each of the cheese rounds.

14. Drizzle each plate with a touch of extra-virgin olive oil. Serve at room temperature.

Pears, blue cheese, and almonds—they're a flavor combination classic. In a new twist here, the pears are poached in brown butter, giving them a nutty, rich flavor that makes the fruit come alive. And compressing the blue cheese makes for a modern presentation that complements your buffet.

Seared Scallops with Spiced Tomato Jam | SERVES 10

INGREDIENTS

10	Scallops, U-10, cleaned
to taste	Kosher salt
to taste	Fresh cracked pepper
1 tbsp / 15 ml	Clarified butter
1/2 cup / 120 ml	Spiced Tomato Jam*
as needed	Extra-virgin olive oil
as needed	Aged balsamic vinegar
as needed	Micro basil

Refer to Appendix A, "From the Chef's Pantry" (p. 204), for this signature recipe.

The sweetness of a pan-seared diver scallop combined with spiced tomato jam is a small-plate creation that will be in demand. The jam can be made days ahead, or even jarred, so it is always on hand.

Method

1. Preheat a heavy-bottom skillet over medium heat for 5 minutes.

2. Dry the scallops thoroughly using a paper towel. Season lightly with kosher salt and pepper.

3. Add the clarified butter to the skillet and wait 1 minute.

4. Add the seasoned scallops to the pan, taking care not to overcrowd them. Cook the scallops on one side until golden brown, approximately 3 minutes.

5. Using tongs, turn the scallops over and continue to cook for an additional 2–3 minutes, until golden brown on the second side.

6. Remove the cooked scallops from the pan and drain on a paper towel.

7. To serve, place 1 scallop onto each plate and spoon a small amount of tomato jam over the scallops.

8. Lightly drizzle each plate with extra-virgin olive oil and aged balsamic vinegar.

9. Finish each plate with a few sprigs of micro basil. Serve immediately.

Cauliflower Panna Cotta | SERVES 10

INGREDIENTS

8 oz / 225 g	Cauliflower, florets
2 oz / 60 g	Shallots, minced
2 tsp / 10 ml	Olive oil
2 oz / 60 ml	White wine
1 oz / 30 g	Butter, unsalted
8 fl oz / 250 ml	Chicken broth
8 fl oz / 250 ml	Heavy cream
2	Gelatin sheets, softened

Garnish

10	Small cauliflower florets, breaded and fried
1 oz / 30 g	Caviar
to taste	Red sea salt

Method

1. Cut the cauliflower florets into 1/2-in. (1-cm) slices.

2. In a medium saucepan over medium heat, sauté the shallots in the olive oil.

3. Deglaze the pan with the white wine and reduce until dry.

4. Add the cauliflower, butter, and chicken broth and bring to a simmer. Let cook for 20 minutes or until most of the liquid is gone and the cauliflower is tender.

5. Add the cream to the pan and simmer for another 10 minutes.

6. Transfer the mixture to a food processor and blend on high until it is a silky smooth purée.

7. Add the softened gelatin sheets to the warm cauliflower mixture and stir gently until dissolved.

8. Spoon the mixture into 10 ramekins and cover lightly with plastic wrap.

9. Place into the refrigerator for 2 hours, to set.

10. At time of service, remove the ramekins from the refrigerator and garnish each with 1 piece of fried cauliflower, a bit of caviar, and a sprinkle of red sea salt. Serve immediately.

Cauliflower is an underappreciated vegetable, from my point of view. In fact, it lends itself well to many cooking procedures as a flavor partner—lobster, truffles, and caviar, to name just a few. In this panna cotta version, the decadence of caviar joins with crispy cauliflower. The saltiness of the caviar and richness of the cauliflower produce a delicious marriage of flavors for any small plate.

Vegetable-Crusted Scallops | SERVES 10

INGREDIENTS

10	Sea scallops, U-10, cleaned
1 tbsp / 15 ml	Clarified butter
to taste	Kosher salt
to taste	Cracker black pepper
1 cup / 250 ml	Signature Vegetable Crust*

Garnish

10 pieces   Asparagus, cut on bias, blanched

Refer to Appendix A, "From the Chef's Pantry" (p. 203), for this signature recipe.

Method

1. Preheat a heavy-bottom skillet over medium-high heat for 5 minutes.

2. Using a paper towel, dry the scallops thoroughly and then season lightly with kosher salt and pepper.

3. Add the clarified butter to the preheated skillet and wait 1 minute.

4. Add the scallops to the pan, taking care not to overcrowd them.

5. Allow the scallops to cook on one side for 3 minutes. Remove from the pan and place them onto an ovenproof plate, browned side up.

6. Cover the top of the scallops with the vegetable crust.

7. At time of service, place the tray of scallops into a preheated 300°F (150°C) oven for 3 minutes, or until the scallops are cooked to desired doneness.

8. Remove the scallops from the oven and insert 1 piece of the bias-cut asparagus into each scallop.

9. Arrange each scallop on a plate and serve immediately.

Wet-Cured Salmon, Daikon, Orange, and Yuzu | SERVES 6

INGREDIENTS

1 tsp / 5 ml	Olive oil	
1/2 cup / 125 ml	Yuzu juice	
1 tbsp / 15 ml	Fresh parsley, chopped fine	
6–8 oz / 165–225 g	Salmon	
as needed	Kosher salt	
as needed	Fresh cracked pepper	

1 tbsp / 15 ml	Orange zest
1/2 tsp / 2 ml	Rice vinegar
3 tbsp / 45 ml	Daikon, shredded
3 tsp / 15 ml	Seaweed salad
as needed	Black sea salt

Method

1. In a small bowl, combine the olive oil, 2 tbsp (30 ml) yuzu juice, and parsley. Mix well to combine.

2. Lightly pound the salmon, shaping into an even square. Season with kosher salt and fresh cracked pepper. Add to the yuzu mixture and toss to coat well.

3. Lay a sheet of plastic wrap onto your work surface and place the marinated salmon onto it.

4. Wrap the salmon tightly in the plastic, to form a uniform log. Tie ends tightly with twine to secure, and place into the refrigerator overnight.

5. In small bowl, combine the remaining yuzu juice, orange zest, and rice vinegar. Mix well to combine; season to taste with kosher salt and black pepper. Place into the refrigerator until time of service.

6. At time of service, arrange 6 service vessels onto your work surface. Place an equal portion of shredded daikon into the center of each. Divide the seaweed salad evenly and array around the shredded daikon.

7. Remove the salmon from the refrigerator and slice into 6 equal portions. Place 1 piece on top of each pile of shredded daikon.

8. Divide the orange and yuzu mixture evenly among of the vessels.

9. Finish each plate with a light sprinkling of black sea salt. Serve well chilled.

Cured and smoked salmon are staples at delis, brunches, and many buffets. For this small plate, the salmon is cured with the tantalizing flavor of yuzu juice. (A yuzu is about the size of a tangerine and has an aroma and flavor distinct from any other citrus fruit, though somewhat akin to a cross between a grapefruit and lime.) The recipe marries daikon, orange, and the fish in a one-of-a-kind cured salmon.

This small plate achieves the objective of simple, elegant food. Lobster stuffed into cauliflower, with sweet pea purée underneath and garnished with crispy sweetbreads, is a showcase dish for any buffet.

Lobster-Stuffed Cauliflower, Sweet Pea Purée, and Crispy Sweet Breads | SERVES 10

INGREDIENTS

5	Baby cauliflower heads		2	Whole eggs, whipped lightly
as needed	Milk		1 cup / 225 ml	Fine panko bread crumbs
10 oz / 285 g	Lobster Mousse*		1 cup / 225 ml	Fresh peas, blanched
1 cup / 225 ml	All-purpose flour		6	Large spinach leaves, stems removed
to taste	Kosher salt		1 cup / 250 ml	Chicken stock
to taste	Fresh cracked pepper		2 tbsp / 30 ml	Unsalted butter
10 each	Sweetbread morsels, blanched and peeled		to taste	Black sea salt

*Refer to Appendix A, "From the Chef's Pantry" (p. 201), for this signature recipe.

Method

1. Remove any green leaves from the bottom of the baby cauliflower and place heads into a stainless-steel saucepan. Add enough milk to cover the cauliflower by 1 in. (2.5 cm).

2. Place the pan over medium heat and bring to a simmer. Continue to simmer until the cauliflower is fork-tender, approximately 10 minutes.

3. Remove the cauliflower from the milk and allow to cool in the refrigerator.

4. Once cooled, use a small knife to remove the stem and center from the cauliflower.

5. Lay a large square of plastic wrap onto your work surface. Place 1 cauliflower head upside down in the center of the plastic. Place 2 oz (60 g) of the lobster mousse into the center of the cauliflower.

6. Grab the four corners of the plastic, pull around the cauliflower, and twist tight. Using a piece of twine, tie the plastic in place.

7. Repeat until all of the cauliflower heads are stuffed and wrapped. Reserve the stuffed cauliflower in the refrigerator until time of service.

8. Season the flour with kosher salt and pepper. Add the sweetbread morsels to the seasoned flour and toss to coat evenly.

9. Remove the sweetbreads from the flour and place into the whipped eggs; toss to coat evenly.

10. Remove the sweetbreads from the egg and add to the fine panko; toss to coat evenly. Remove and reserve for service.

11. Place the blanched peas, spinach, and chicken stock into a small stainless-steel saucepan; bring to a boil and then simmer for 3 minutes.

12. Pour the heated mixture into a Vitamix® blender and purée until smooth. Season with kosher salt and pepper. Add the butter and purée again. Reserve warm for service.

13. At time of service, place the wrapped cauliflower heads into simmering water and cook until they reach an internal temperature of 140°F (60°C). Take from the water and remove plastic wrap.

14. Cut each head of cauliflower in half and place a half onto each of the service plates.

15. Fry the breaded sweetbreads in a preheated 350°F (175°C) deep fryer until golden brown. Remove from the fryer, drain on a paper towel, and season lightly with kosher salt.

16. Spoon a small amount of the warm pea purée onto each plate, followed by a crispy sweetbread.

17. Finish each plate with a touch of black sea salt. Serve immediately.

CHAPTER NINE

THE ART AND TASTE OF PASTRY

Pastry, for many buffet fans, is the highlight of the display. As such, it offers an opportunity for the pastry chef to create centerpieces that showcase his or her artistic talent. While pastry does not present the same challenges that savory food does, as with any buffet food, how desserts taste is the ultimate determinant of success. And with pastry especially, a tempting display must be matched by rich flavor and texture. For customers, nothing is more disappointing than partaking of a treat that has caught their eye, but, when tasted, does not live up to expectations.

It is the combination of presentation and great taste that makes buffet desserts and pastries impossible for guests to resist, from a humble yet delicious apple pie to the fanciest parfaits and chocolate concoctions. Using seasonal fruits and flavors is one way to ensure that flavor profiles are at their optimum; and adding a garnish of chocolate, sugar, glazed fruits, and other items can enhance the

An elegant pastry display, buffet style. The wide assortment of pastries assures there is something for everyone. The centerpiece complements but does not dominate, and the use of different service vessels, at a variety of heights, produces a stunning overall effect.

simplest desserts. Similarly, varying display heights and service vessels adds to the elegance and the enticing look of any buffet.

Another key to a successful pastry buffet is to offer something for everyone. Chocolate, for example, is a crowd favorite, and a natural to work with, but there are guests who do not care for chocolate, who prefer fruit flavors or vanilla desserts instead. This fact allows the pastry chef to expand his or her repertoire further, adding jellies, candies, meringues, puddings, classical cakes, cookies, and more. The dessert menu is limited only by an individual's imagination and ability.

Pastry Buffet

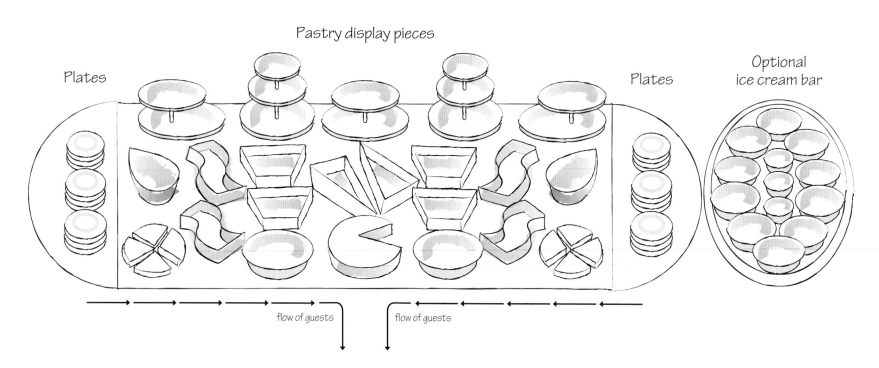

Pastry display pieces

Plates

Plates

Optional ice cream bar

flow of guests   flow of guests

Like other buffet types, pastry buffets, too, can be designed around a specific theme, depending on the event or occasion. For example, a fifties-theme night might suggest a milkshake bar, pies (apple, cherry, lemon meringue, banana cream), and donuts. There is, however, one rule of thumb to follow when creating a pastry buffet: No matter how large or small the selections, put them on their own table, separate from the main savory food items.

For those operations that do not have the resources to maintain a large pastry department, there are companies that sell centerpiece kits, premade pastry display pieces, and all types of pastry, from bite-size to full-size desserts and everything in between.

The photos here illustrate a number of pastry buffets, from themed to full-service. They give you a firsthand look at how a variety of pastries and serving vessels can come together in a buffet that is both wonderful to look at and guaranteed to end the meal on a high note.

A closer view shows how creative this buffet setup is. The pastries, varying in flavor, shape, texture, and presentation, are sure to exceed guest expectations.

Another reason small bites are ideal for pastry buffets is that they show off a variety of colors, textures, shapes, and tempting flavors.

This simple and elegant presentation of French macaroons makes for a very attractive addition to a buffet.

This rich torte, which can be made in a variety of shapes, is served at room temperature so it melts on the tongue. A touch of gold leaf lends an elegant finishing touch.

Chocolate Torte | SERVES 8

INGREDIENTS

4	Eggs
6	Egg yolks
1 lb / 450 g	Dark chocolate
12 oz / 340 g	Butter
1/2 sheet pan	Tart Dough*

*Refer to Appendix A, "From the Chef's Pantry" (p. 205), for this signature recipe.

Method

1. Mix eggs and egg yolks over a double boiler until warm.

2. In a separate saucepan, melt the butter and add the chocolate. Mix until well incorporated. Set aside.

3. Place egg mixture into mixer. Whip until tripled in volume.

4. Once the egg mixture has reached proper consistency, slowly pour in the chocolate butter mixture.

5. Pour this batter into par-baked tart dough shell.

6. Place into 325°F (165°C) oven and bake for 15 minutes.

7. Remove from oven let cool for 15 minutes then place into the refrigerator overnight.

8. Cut into small bar pieces when ready to serve.

9. Bring to room temperature and serve.

Chocolate Caramel Ganache Tarts | SERVES 8

INGREDIENTS

8 fl oz / 250 ml   Heavy cream

1 lb / 450 g   Dark chocolate

1 fl oz / 30 ml   Kahlua

8   Tart Shells*, 2 in. (5 cm)

4 oz / 125 ml   Dulce de leche

Chocolate ganache

1 cup / 250 ml Heavy cream

1-1/2 cup / 315 ml Semisweet chocolate, chopped or chips

3 tbsp / 45 ml Butter, cold

Refer to Appendix A, "From the Chef's Pantry" (p. 205), for this signature recipe.

Chocolate and caramel is a match made in heaven. These finger food pastries may be small, but they are big on flavor. To spice up this recipe and give it a great yin-and-yang flavor, add a touch of sea salt on top of the caramel.

Method

1. Place heavy cream in pot and bring to a simmer.

2. Once cream is ready, fold in chocolate and Kahlua.

3. Mix until smooth.

4. While the mixture is still warm, fill each tart shell.

5. To prepare the ganache, in a stainless steel sauce pan, bring the heavy cream to a boil; reduce to a simmer and simmer for 3 minutes.

6. Remove the pan from heat and whisk in the chocolate. Once chocolate has melted, whisk in butter.

7. Cool ganache in the refrigerator. When ready to use, whisk until fluffy.

8. Using a piping bag, squeeze a small amount of dulce de leche on top of each tart. Decorate with cooled chocolate ganache.

Crème brûlée is a dessert classic, but in these bite-size versions, it becomes something more, thanks to the addition of a blackberry and French macaroon.

Crème Brûlée | SERVES 8

INGREDIENTS

2 cups / 500 ml	Heavy cream
1	Vanilla bean
4	Egg yolks
3 oz / 85 g	Granulated sugar
6 oz / 170 g	Sugar in the raw

Method

1. In a heavy-bottom stainless-steel saucepan, heat cream with vanilla bean over medium-low heat for 15 minutes, stirring to ensure it does not burn.

2. Remove from heat and let steep for 15 minutes. Remove and discard the vanilla bean.

3. In a mixing bowl, blend the egg yolks with the granulated sugar until well incorporated.

4. Temper in the egg mixture with cream. Cook until slightly thicker.

5. Fill each service spoon with the brûlée and place on a baking tray with a water bath.

6. Place tray in the oven and bake in a 300°F (150°C) until set.

7. Remove from oven and place in refrigerator to continue setting and until cool.

8. When ready to serve, sprinkle the crème brûlée with the raw sugar and torch the sugar using a blow torch until the sugar has caramelized. Serve immediately.

9. Decorate with your favorite garnishes.

Hazelnut Cake Layers | SERVES 8

INGREDIENTS

1 sheet   Hazelnut Cake*

2 lb / 900 g   Coffee Buttercream*

8 fl oz / 250 ml   Heavy cream

1 lb / 450 g   Dark chocolate

Refer to Appendix A, "From the Chef's Pantry" (p. 193, 198), for these signature recipes.

Method

1. Cut hazelnut cake lengthwise into 3 equal parts.

2. Spread buttercream evenly on first part of cake; lay the second part of cake on top of the first, and repeat this process one more time. Place the cake layers into refrigerator until ready to garnish.

3. To make the ganache, heat the heavy cream in a small pot.

4. Mix in the dark chocolate until well incorporated. Cool.

5. Spread the ganache on the top cake layer and smooth it out with an offset spatula. Place back in refrigerator until the ganache sets.

6. When ready to serve, use a hot knife to cut through the cake layers.

7. Garnish with toasted hazelnuts or hazelnuts dipped in caramel sugar.

Hazelnut is a delectable flavor that is even better paired with chocolate. These bars contain a trio of flavors: hazelnut cake, coffee buttercream, and rich ganache—sinfully good.

Strawberry Pâte de Fruit | SERVES 8

INGREDIENTS

1/2 oz / 15 g	Pectin
8 oz / 225 g	Granulated sugar
7 oz / 210 g	Strawberry purée, warm
3–1/2 oz / 90 g	Glucose
1/2 oz / 15 g	Citric acid
as needed	Sugar, superfine
8	Strawberry slices

A true pâte de fruit is not chewy, but a soft yet firm jelly whose burst of flavor excites the palate.

Strawberry jellies have a sweet-and-sour flavor that melts in your mouth. These skewers are accented with a slice of fresh strawberry.

Method

1. Using a small pot, mix the pectin with 1 oz (30 g) of sugar.

2. Add the warm purée to the mixture in stages, to prevent lumps.

3. Bring to a boil. Add the glucose to the mixture and bring to a second boil, and then simmer for 4 minutes

4. Add the remaining sugar and bring to a third boil, then simmer for another 5 minutes.

5. Add the citric acid and boil until temperature reaches 220°F (106°C).

6. When right temperature is reached, pour into desired molds.

7. Leave molds to sit overnight, at room temp to set.

8. When ready for service, cut into desired shape then toss pieces in superfine sugar, to prevent a skin forming on the pâté de fruit.

9. Insert the pieces on skewers or picks, followed by a slice of fresh strawberry.

Praline Almond Layer Cake | SERVES 16

INGREDIENTS

1 sheet   Frangipane*

2 lb / 900 g   Hazelnut Buttercream*

1 lb / 450 g   Basic Buttercream*

16   Chocolate garnishes

Refer to Appendix A, "From the Chef's Pantry" (p. 193, 198), for these signature recipes.

Method

1. Cut the frangipane sheet into 5 equal parts.

2. Spread the hazelnut buttercream evenly on one layer of the cake. Set the second cake layer on top of it; repeat the process one more time, alternating buttercream flavors until all layers are done.

3. Put the cake into the refrigerator overnight. When ready for use, cut with a hot knife into desired shapes.

4. Using a round tip, pipe decorative rounds of plain buttercream on top of cake, to hold chocolate garnish.

This praline cake adds another dimension to any buffet selection. Filled with two types of buttercream, it makes an elegant selection for those who may not be fans of chocolate.

Chocolate Mousse | **SERVES 8**

INGREDIENTS

8 fl oz / 250 ml   Heavy cream

6 oz / 170 g   Dark chocolate

2 oz / 60 g   Egg yolks

4–1/2 oz / 130 g   Granulated sugar

2–1/2 oz / 75 g   Egg whites

1 fl oz / 30 ml   Brandy

Chocolate mousse is always a favorite on dessert buffets. This one is given a new twist by chilling it in a mold then spraying it lightly with powdered chocolate, to give it a more finished look and add texture. The garnish is cream with a macaroon, for a nice crunch.

Method

1. Whip the heavy cream to a firm peak; reserve in the refrigerator.

2. Melt the chocolate over a double boiler.

3. Heat the egg yolks and half of the sugar over another double boiler. Whip constantly to prevent overheating. The egg yolk mixture must reach 145°F (65°C).

4. In a bowl, whip the egg whites while gradually adding the remaining sugar. Whip to a medium peak.

5. Fold the chocolate into the whipped yolk mixture, and then add the brandy.

6. Fold the whipped cream into the chocolate mixture.

7. Add the whipped meringue into the chocolate mixture. Do not overfold.

8. Pipe into dome molds, all the way to the top.

9. Set in freezer overnight.

10. Once frozen, remove the mousse from the molds. Keep in the refrigerator until ready to serve.

11. Garnish with dollop of whipped cream, macaroon, and a chocolate cigarette.

Fresh Fruit Tart | SERVES 8

INGREDIENTS

2 cups / 500 ml	Whole milk
6 oz / 170 g	Granulated sugar
pinch	Salt
3/4 oz / 22 g	Cornstarch
1/4 oz / 7 g	Cake flour
3 oz / 90 ml	Egg yolks

1–1/2 oz / 45 ml	Whole eggs
to taste	Vanilla extract
1–1/2 oz / 45 g	Butter, unsalted
8	Tart Shells*, 4 in. (10 cm)
as needed	Assortment of fruit to display on tarts
8 fl oz / 250 ml	Apricot glaze

*Refer to Appendix A, "From the Chef's Pantry" (p. 205), for this signature recipe.

Method

1. Place 3/4 of the milk, 1/2 the sugar, and salt into a pot and bring to a boil.

2. Place the cornstarch, remaining sugar, and flour into a mixing bowl and mix until incorporated; add the remaining milk, to help form a smooth paste.

3. Add the egg yolks and eggs to the cornstarch mixture.

4. Temper the cornstarch mixture. Add to the boiling milk.

5. Bring the mixture to a second boil, stirring constantly; cook for 3 minutes.

6. Remove from heat and stir in the vanilla and butter. Whisk well.

7. Cool properly and refrigerate.

8. After the pastry cream has cooled, fill each tart shell 3/4 of way up.

9. Arrange fruit attractively on top of pastry cream.

10. When ready to serve, apply apricot glaze

Fresh fruit tarts are pastry favorites. The most important rule for making successful fruit tarts is to use the freshest fruit available and high-quality pastry cream made with real vanilla. The glaze is optional; you can leave the tarts plain, or sprinkle powdered sugar on the fruit before service.

Lemon has outstanding flavor, and this recipe balances its tartness with the sweetness of meringue. This is another example of simplicity at its best.

Lemon Meringue Tart | SERVES 8

INGREDIENTS

1–3/4 oz / 40 g	Cornstarch
1 qt / 1 L	Water
4 oz / 125 ml	Eggs
6 oz / 170 g	Granulated sugar
to taste	Salt
1–1/2	Lemon rinds, grated
5 tbsp / 75 ml	Fresh lemon juice
1 oz / 30 g	Butter
8	Tart Shells*, 4 in. (10 cm)
1 lb / 450 g	Italian Meringue*
8 chocolate garnishes	

*Refer to Appendix A, "From the Chef's Pantry" (p. 200, 205), for these signature recipes.

Method

1. Place the cornstarch in a bowl; slowly add 1 fl oz (30 ml) of water and whisk until dissolved. There should be no lumps in the mixture.

2. Add the eggs to the cornstarch mixture.

3. In a pot, combine the remaining water with the sugar, salt, and lemon; bring to a boil.

4. At boiling, temper the cornstarch mixture and add to the hot mixture.

5. Bring to a second boil and allow mixture to thicken, approximately 3 to 5 minutes.

6. Remove from heat; add lemon juice and butter.

7. Pour into tart shells; put them into refrigerator to set.

8. Using a small round tip on a piping bag, garnish the top of the tart shells with the Italian meringue.

9. Bake the tarts until the meringue turns brown; or use a propane torch to brown the meringue. Garnish, if desired, with pressed chocolate ribbon or a sprinkle of gold leaf.

Mango Mousse | SERVES 8

INGREDIENTS

1/4 oz / 7 g	Gelatin
1–1/4 oz / 37 g	Water
9–1/2 oz / 285 g	Mango purée
1 qt / 1 L	Heavy cream
2 oz / 60 g	Confectionary sugar
8 oz / 225 ml	Mango Gelée*
1 cup / 250 ml	Heavy cream, whipped
8	Chocolate buttons
8	Strips of chocolate or 8 Candied mangos

Refer to Appendix A, "From the Chef's Pantry" (p. 202), for this signature recipe.

Method

1. Place the gelatin in a dry bowl and bloom with water.

2. Melt the bloomed gelatin over a double boiler.

3. Add the fruit purée to the gelatin.

4. Allow the mixture to cool.

5. Whip the heavy cream and sugar to a medium peak.

6. Gently fold together the whipped cream and fruit purée mixture.

7. Pipe the mousse into prepared molds and allow to set.

8. Once set, pour the gelée over the mousse. Let it set in the refrigerator until service time.

9. Remove the mousse from the molds.

10. Pipe a dollop of whipped cream on top of the mousse and then decorate with chocolate button garnish and chocolate strip; or use diced candied mangos.

This fruit mousse offers an alternative to the usual chocolate or vanilla variety. The gelée on top adds a really nice contrast to both presentation and flavor.

Carrot Cake | SERVES 8

INGREDIENTS

2 lb 2 oz / 960 g Bread flour

1–1/4 oz / 35 g Baking powder

3/4 oz / 22 g Baking soda

3/4 oz / 22 g Cinnamon, ground

1/2 oz / 15 g Salt

1/4 oz / 7 g Nutmeg, ground

2 lb 7oz / 1.1 kg Granulated sugar

2 qt / 2 L Vegetable oil

1 lb 8 oz / 1.25 L Whole eggs

12 oz / 340 g Raisins

2 lb 4 oz / 1 kg Carrots, shredded

2 lb / 1 kg Cream cheese frosting

8 Marzipan carrots (for garnish)

8 pieces Gold leaf

8 Chocolate fans

How do you take carrot cake to the next level? Make it as individual portions and garnish with a marzipan carrot, a touch of gold leaf, and white chocolate.

The advantage to individual-size cakes is no mess on the buffet and no unfinished cake sitting there looking unappetizing.

Method

1. Sift together the bread flour, baking powder, baking soda, cinnamon, salt, and nutmeg.

2. Place the granulated sugar and oil in a second bowl; combine by mixing with a paddle.

3. To the sugar and oil mixture slowly add the eggs, in stages, to combine.

4. Add the sifted ingredients to the wet ingredients.

5. Fold in the raisins and shredded carrots.

6. Fill 8 3-in. (8-cm) cake pans. Bake for 20 minutes at 350°F (175°C), or until golden brown.

7. Cool the cakes and then fill and ice with cream cheese frosting. Keep refrigerated until needed.

8. On each cake, place a marzipan or piped buttercream carrot, along with some gold leaf and a chocolate fan.

New York Cheesecake | SERVES 8

INGREDIENTS

6 oz / 185 ml   Butter, melted

1 lb / 450 g   Graham cracker crumbs

1 lb 8 oz / 675 g   Cream cheese

1 tsp / 5 ml   Lemon rind, grated

8 oz / 225 g   Granulated sugar

4 fl oz / 125 ml   Heavy cream

8 oz / 250 ml   Whole eggs

1 oz / 30 ml   Sour cream

2 fl oz / 60 ml   Half-and-half

to taste   Vanilla extract

There's not much you can say about rich and creamy New York-style cheesecake that hasn't already been said. But when it comes to including this favorite on a buffet, the same principle applies: Present it in small tasting or individual portions, to prevent the mess of unfinished whole cakes. Fresh fruit topping is all that is needed to add to success here.

Method

1. To prepare the crust, preheat oven to 350°F (175°C). Mix the butter and graham cracker crumbs together; press mixture into bottom of 9-in. (23-cm) spring-form pan or individual pans. Bake for 10 minutes. Remove and let cool.

2. Place the cream cheese in a bowl with the lemon rind. Paddle until smooth.

3. Add the sugar and paddle until smooth, scraping often.

4. Add the heavy cream, continuing to paddle and scrape down the bowl.

5. Add the eggs in small amounts, incorporating well after each addition. Scrape the bowl well.

6. Add the sour cream, half-and-half, and vanilla extract.

7. Pour the mixture into the prepared pans. Place the pans on a tray within water bath and place in oven.

8. Bake at 225°F (110°C) for 1 hour or until the centers are firm.

9. Remove from oven and cool.

10. To garnish, use a variety of fresh fruit compotes or marinated fresh-cut fruits or berries; candied lemon or orange slices; or, simply, a dollop of whipped cream.

CHAPTER TEN

CLASSIC BUFFETS MADE ELEGANT

*I*n recent years, the introduction of innovative cooking methods, coupled with the fusion of new cuisine flavors, has created many opportunities for the industry and customers alike. Yet no matter how many changes take place within the culinary arts, the classics and old favorites never go out of style, regardless of the venue. Many family restaurant chains made their names on signature classic dishes. Howard Johnson®, for one, became known for its hot dogs, served in grilled New England-style buns, its clam strips, and, of course, its ice cream. Other venues became known not for individual dishes, but rather, for a style of service—in particular, the buffet. Most famously, Las Vegas hotels and casinos drew huge crowds to their buffets. Even today, in spite of all the upscale dining Las Vegas now has to offer, guests still most enjoy the buffets, served at breakfast, lunch, and dinner all across the city. True, many of these have been revamped

in recent years, both in presentation and selection of food, but as the saying goes, "The more things change, the more they remain the same."

The resurgence of comfort food in the first decade of the twenty-first century, on both à la carte and buffet menus, came in response to customer demand—it was what they missed and wanted. To meet that demand, chefs have found new ways to serve and present such homey dishes as meatloaf, pot roast, mashed potatoes, and the like, which are not only infused with rich flavor but are rich in memories and tradition, as well. Sunday brunch without eggs Benedict or an omelet station wouldn't be Sunday brunch to guests, who expect to see those "regulars" on the menu, regardless of the other food being offered. Fortunately, for chefs, the versatility of food makes it possible to respect tradition and offer classic dishes while at the same time putting a modern twist on them, both in terms of flavor profiles and presentation. Eggs Benedict, as you saw in Chapter 2, "Sensational Breakfasts," becomes even more interesting when prepared in alternative versions, such as with lobster, short ribs, or spinach, taking this familiar dish to a new level.

The objective of this chapter is to demonstrate how longtime customer buffet favorites can, with just a few modifications, be elevated to new heights, and add a touch of elegance to any buffet, in any venue, and for any occasion.

EGGS BENEDICT

Just because eggs Benedict is a perennially popular buffet brunch and breakfast favorite doesn't mean it's easy to produce from the chef's point of view. It is always a challenge to poach the eggs correctly and prevent the hollandaise from drying out, to meet the expectations of the guest.

One option for maintaining the high quality of your eggs Benedict on your buffet is to prepare them at an action station. In this way, you can ensure freshness while also giving you the opportunity to create a variety of benedicts that will get rave reviews from your guests, such as the versions presented in Chapter 2.

You can either poach the eggs to order or you can prepoach them softly and then finish the dish in front of the guests. And give your guests a selection of fresh ingredients to choose from, in addition to the traditional Canadian bacon; this will please both the vegetarians as well as those who enjoy seafood and other meats. It's also a good idea to provide alternatives to the traditional hollandaise sauce, to add to guest enjoyment while complementing the Benedict varieties on the menu. Finally, don't forget to offer your guests a variety of toppings, along with a basket of nicely toasted and enticing English muffins.

The eggs Benedict station can also be presented traditional buffet style, by using grill tops, heat lamps, and heatproof vessels, rather than traditional chafers, which tend to ruin the eggs.

OMELETS

An omelet station is the most popular on a buffet during brunch and breakfast meal periods. For guests, eggs cooked to order, with their selection of ingredients to fold into the eggs, is hard to pass up. Today's guests love choice—not to mention being able to have food cooked "their way." The most successful buffets today offer that choice, with a focus on presentation—featuring smaller service vessels that are replaced more often, to ensure freshness, and stations staffed by chefs who plate the food or cook it to order for the guest.

The omelet station, though simple in concept, can be made to look truly elegant with very little effort:

- Use covers to disguise the portable butane burners.

- Display the bowls for fillings on black slate boards, to add a nice contrast.

- Put a bowl of fresh eggs on the table for those who prefer fried eggs rather than an omelet.

- Set up a bin with ice draped in linens, to hold bain-maries of pasteurized eggs and egg whites, for those who desire a healthier option.

One effective presentation concept is to arrange bowls attractively around the burner, so that it is easier for the attendant to reach the fillings, while also giving the customers a clear view of their choices.

As noted, an omelet station should, of course, feature multiple fillings for the guest to choose from. At the same time, it's important to carefully balance the number of choices on buffet stations that feature cooked-to-order food, for the simple reason that the greater the choice, the harder the decision will be for the guests to make, and this can cause line backups during peak hours. The rule of thumb for action stations is roughly 1 station per 80 guests. So, a buffet function of 160 people would most likely feature 2 omelet stations, for efficient service.

CLASSIC BARBEQUE

Barbeque is a favorite everywhere. Guests love the aroma and taste of spicy, smoky, and sweet—whether tender ribs, pulled pork, sliced brisket, chicken, or seafood. The backdrop to a barbeque buffet station is the smoker in which the barbeque items are cooked. If you are fortunate to have a smoker of any type for an outside buffet, it will add an element of authenticity to the presentation. In many cases, however, the barbequed foods are produced the day before and then reheated or finished in the smoker. The smoker then becomes a holding box for the food; nevertheless, the smell emanating from it will attract attention to the station and give it that wow factor so important to any buffet.

Rather than serve baked macaroni and cheese from a chafer dish, put it in a ceramic heatproof casserole dish under a heat lamp and hot grill, to give a rustic feel to this. The brisket is ready for carving, while ribs, chicken, and pulled pork promise to make this a barbeque that will have guests talking all night long! Note the wooden carving board, a small but important detail.

It is not necessary to spend a lot of money to produce that wow factor, by the way. For example, a large cast-iron pan transforms baked beans into an inviting side dish. No silver or SS burner covers? Slates of stone are very attractive and effective for covering burners; and, at an outside function, they can also aid in deflecting the wind and helping to maintain the full heat of the flame.

The little things, done correctly, complete the picture of any buffet. A slow-cooked ham, smoked fresh, remains in a holder for easy carving and adds a nice touch to the buffet display. xsA friendly face offering grilled corn, baked beans, and hot, smoked barbequed salmon pleases guests, makes your action station more inviting, and does not add to your costs.

MEXICAN

The simplest foods can sometimes be the most difficult to present well on a buffet station. Many ethnic foods, such as the Mexican cuisine described here, are the most flavorful and have major customer appeal and popularity, but too often are not displayed to good effect. Leaving food sitting out for too long is a common mistake; it gives the wrong impression of the cuisine and guests will stay away.

Whether feeding 50, 100, 200 people, or more, with a little effort and out-of-the-box thinking, it's possible to make any type of buffet elegant and appealing—one that you and your team can be proud of. The Mexican station is really a simple one, in that the menu consists of some standard offerings: two types of tacos, tamales, spiced lime shrimp, rice, refried beans, salsa, chips, and other accoutrements.

The Mexican buffet comes alive with the help of Sterno grills, heat lamps, black cast-iron pans for the hot food, a nice basket for the chips, square glass containers for the salsas, wooden risers, a stone pesto bowl for the guacamole, and a blue glass plate for the lettuce and tomato. All simple in design, but when placed together create a stunning effect.

CREATE EXCITEMENT

The classic buffet stations described in this chapter—eggs Benedict, omelet, barbeque, and Mexican—are just four of many, used to demonstrate that to be successful, all buffets, from the simplest to the most complex, depend on the same elements: correct preparation, correct selection of ingredients, correct planning and layout of the buffet, correct display items to complement the food on display, and, finally, correct attention to guests.

This chapter also makes the important point that any classic buffet can be revamped to meet modern tastes and preferences, in food and presentation design. Here are some tips that will help you make every buffet you develop a winner. Buffet excitement and pride can be achieved with a little work and effort from all involved.

- Feature add-ons to the stations for greater appeal and customer convenience. Placing Danish, muffins, and fruit parfaits, for example, on your omelet station or hot breakfast buffet adds not only greater variety, but color and depth to the presentation, as well.

- Use props, risers, different-shape china, textured linens, and tabletops to give style to even the most basic buffet.

- Once you find the right look for a buffet, take a digital picture of it before the guests arrive; and when the buffet is over, pack all the props and decorations in a box or plastic container, with a detailed label describing its contents. Finally, tape the picture on the outside of the box/container, to make it easy for anyone to re-create the presentation to the same high standard for subsequent events.

- Remember, less is more—and better—on a buffet! Smaller plates of food refilled often ensure that the last guest will receive the same high-quality food and service as the first.

- Let guests build their meals. Hamburgers and hotdogs, for example, served from a chafer may be convenient, but they do not hold well, and their quality will be questionable, at best. Instead, array them in vessels on a grill with heat lamps, and arrange baskets of rolls and condiments nearby.

In the end, food is always the most important thing at any event, meeting, or celebration that requires a buffet service. Whether they've been listening to speeches, dancing, or celebrating a family occasion, people will get hungry; they will want to eat. Make sure the food you display and serve on your buffet is special, always.

CHAPTER ELEVEN

DINE-AROUND BUFFETS

The dine-around buffet raises the classic buffet to a new level. In its most simplistic form, the dine-around buffet takes the traditional large-table setup, on which the entire buffet was spread (the *grand buffet*, as it was called), and reconfigures it as several individual buffets, using smaller tables and food displays arranged logically around the venue. This approach allows guests to walk around and dine (hence, "dine around"), improving the flow of both traffic and service and alleviating the congestion that typically forms when everything is in one place. The dine-around buffet also breaks with tradition in terms of serving vessels, moving away from large to smaller platters and/or plates that are refreshed more often so that the food always looks fresh, no matter what time the guest approaches.

Dine-around stations can be staffed or self-serve, depending on the labor model. The advantage of a chef-staffed station is twofold: one, the opportunity to interact with the guests, and, two, better portion control of the food. A station featuring a shrimp dish, for example, will be better managed if there's a chef behind the station serving the food, as opposed to letting guests help themselves.

Another advantage of the dine-around buffet is food cost savings. You can put out the end products in batches, as needed; and when the buffet is over, any leftover food, stored properly in the kitchen, can be used as fresh product on other days and for other purposes.

A traditional dine-around station provides a variety of selections that can handle small to medium buffets and for a larger amount of guests just duplicate in another room.

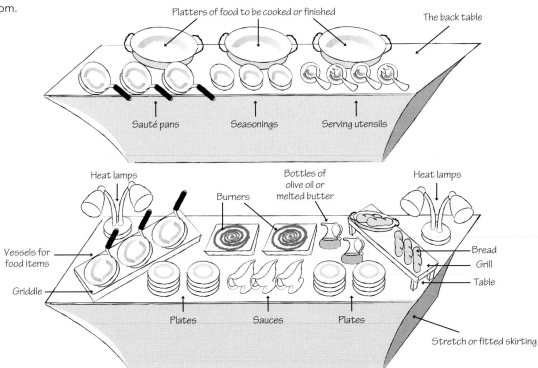

Action Station
(for dine-around buffet)

Platters of food to be cooked or finished

The back table

Sauté pans

Seasonings

Serving utensils

Heat lamps

Burners

Bottles of olive oil or melted butter

Heat lamps

Vessels for food items

Bread

Grill

Table

Griddle

Plates

Sauces

Plates

Stretch or fitted skirting

A dine-around buffet is versatile, as well; the number buffet stations it has will depend on the total number of guests expected. A party of 300, for example, would most likely require 2 of every station to accommodate the flow and to serve the guests in a reasonable amount of time. Popular stations may, of course, need more attention. A brunch for 260 might include 3 omelet buffet stations or 3 double stations.

The dine-around buffet also offers greater flexibility for the chef in terms of the menu, making it possible to include new and fun concepts, such as a fondue station and a Chicago steak house, both described more fully later in this chapter. One of the most popular stations I have developed is for Peking duck, where a chef is on hand to pull tender, slow-roasted duck, place it into a pancake that has been flavored with a sauce, and then roll it into a two- to three-bite wrap. It is, simply, too much for guests to resist.

When it comes to decorating dine-around buffet stations, you want to be sure that each table coordinates appropriately with the station. Let the décor speak for the table and add value to the main buffet menu item featured. For example, a simple pasta station on which are arrayed cheesy garlic bread, grated parmesan cheese, crushed red pepper, a good olive oil, perhaps even a Caesar salad, will be a winner.

In sum, a dine-around buffet is the complete package, and the concept and design options are unlimited. Here are just a few to get your creative juices flowing.

CHICAGO STEAK HOUSE

What meat lover does not enjoy a good steak house? You will delight your guests by creating the same atmosphere at a buffet station. A steak house buffet is also very "user-friendly," in that the client selecting the menu for an event cannot fail to succeed if it features creamed spinach, miniature baked potatoes with all the fixins', sautéed mushrooms and onions, steak house salad, carved flank steak, house-made steak sauce, Parker House rolls, and assorted dressings.

The scope and expense of this buffet station can be adjusted to the customer's budget. You can carve rib-eye steaks, New York sirloins, prime rib, flat iron, or other cuts to accommodate your customer. You can also substitute the steak house salad with a Caesar; add creamed corn—the possibilities are endless.

Always popular with customers is the classic chopped steak house salad composed of iceberg lettuce, diced sharp cheese, olives, cucumbers, diced tomatoes, croutons, and red onions. Add Parker House rolls and it becomes a buffet in and of itself.

Carved flank steak, creamed spinach, petite baked potatoes, mushrooms and onions, plus all the fixins' make this buffet a winner.

BISTRO STATION

The French bistro is a casual venue in which diners can enjoy simple, delicious fare. Bistro food is considered by many as comfort food in the form of classic French dishes that also offer value for the money.

The bistro buffet, as with all buffet stations, should offer simple, well-prepared, and tasty food that is recognizable to the customer and features accoutrements that carry out the theme. The bistro menu should include two to three hot dishes, such as chicken coq au vin, roasted salmon mignons, or even petite filets with pommes frites. Two or three composed and uncomposed salads that complement the main offerings also should also be presented. Accompany the main items with crispy baguettes, the best butter, pickled vegetables, olive oil and vinegar, along with light dressings, and you will have a station that will exceed even the most discriminating guest's expectations.

Serve this simple bistro salad of mixed greens with endive, corn chips, and pickled vegetables with a red wine dressing.

FONDUE STATION

A Swiss style of cuisine, fondue has made fans all over the world, and adds fun to any gathering. For the chef, a fondue buffet station is a creative opportunity, at the same time it is practical, in that it can handle large volumes of guests. The successful fondue station will have something for everyone: a large vegetarian selection, seafood, meats, and other choices in a format that is simple in nature, user-friendly, and features the one thing people enjoy most about buffets: choice.

Crispy ravioli, broccoli, and fried shrimp, with a variety of fondue sauces, are just a few items that can be included on a fondue buffet.

On their own or as a foundation for other items, pretzel bread and baguettes are musts on a fondue station.

TRATTORIA STATION

The trattoria is the Italian version of the French bistro—classic comfort food full of flavor, prepared to perfection in a casual setting that brings people together for friendship and to share good food.

Pasta stations are standard at buffets, whether dine-around style or self-serve. The trattoria buffet breaks the mold of the pasta station by setting out simple fare, including pastas, but in a more elegant style. The formula for success here is similar to that for the bistro buffet station: Feature two to three hot items, a classic salad, a composed salad, and a variety of olives and/ or cheeses. Enhance the trattoria buffet with good Italian bread, such as focaccia or pizzette (a flatbread garnished and baked like pizza then served on a warming tray), and you've got a winner.

Focaccia is traditional trattoria fare and enjoyed by many.

This trattoria buffet station says "elegant simplicity" with Manga fettuccini and shrimp, veal cutlets, and chicken Marsala.

MARTINI STATION

The martini is a favorite cocktail; likewise, martini bars serving food martini-style are popular, enticing guests with creative new ingredients and presentations. The concept is to serve an item together with its accoutrements in a martini glass so that customers can enjoy all the flavors together.

When designing your menu for a martini station, apply the same rule to this buffet station as other types: be creative and sensible. The options are endless; but, again, keep it simple, never losing sight of the fact that all the ingredients will be going into one glass, so the flavors must complement one another.

One of the most popular items for this station is roast turkey, which on your martini menu can be described as "Roast Turkey Served Martini-Style," or come under the heading "Savory Foods Served Martini-Style." Make sure slices or portions are tender, and sliced thin or bite size, as guests will be using only a fork or spoon to eat it, especially if they are standing. This buffet concept also is ideal for braised items, stews, and other foods that go well with a starch, which absorbs the flavorful sauces and juices.

Roast turkey over stuffing with gravy, and short ribs over mashed potatoes, become elegant buffet items when served in a martini glass. Add cranberry relish and orange marmalade for a bit of flavor and contrast to top off these martini-style items.

THAI STATION

Asian cuisine has become increasingly popular with the American dining public. And it's not just Chinese anymore; also gaining widespread acceptance are Thai, Korean, Vietnamese, and other Asian cuisines.

Thai cuisine, because of its strong French influence, is redolent of spices that excite the taste buds and whet the appetite. Thai food also finds a diverse customer base, as it features many healthy and vibrant vegetarian dishes, making it easy to accommodate this fast-growing market. Add accoutrements such as taro chips, fried or baked wontons with a variety of sauces, and spiced vegetable slaws, and you've got a buffet station sure to draw customers.

For service purposes, hot items can be cooked to order, finished off, or placed in ceramic vessels using the small-batch method. To complete the guest experience, be sure to include an array of chili sauces and other hot flavorings on the buffet table so that customers can add their own degree of spiciness. When it comes to fried or crispy selections, these need to be prepared in small batches to ensure quality. Offer noodles, rice, or both, as the base of these dishes. Asian food, for the most part, uses the protein dishes and sauces to flavor bowls of rice and noodles.

Stations such as this Thai variation give the buffet diversity and are a great way to introduce people to new cuisines as they get to choose, ask questions, and taste in smaller portions.

Dine-around buffet stations are more exciting when a chef attendant is on hand to serve the mouthwatering food.

Beef satay with peanut sauce and crispy chili shrimp add flavorful selections to this exciting Thai station.

A display of cold frothy shakes is enhanced by an ice carving, and surrounded by a variety of small-plate and finger pastries.

MILKSHAKE BAR

As I noted in Chapter 9, "The Art and Taste of Pastry," the dessert station tends to be the highlight of any buffet, the dine-around type included. Typically, at the dine-around pastry station, chefs or cooks attend the station to finish off a tasty treat, help serve guests, and explain the various items on display.

One of the most successful dessert stations I have developed is the milkshake bar. A diner and soda fountain favorite for generations, it made complete sense to take this easy-to-prepare concoction of ice cream, milk, and flavorings to a new level. The first was an adult version for an after-wedding party. On it were featured liqueurs such as Bailey's Irish Cream, Kahlua, and others similar, to jazz up the shakes a bit.

Other ideas to add excitement to a milkshake bar include:

- Use an ice carving to hold the glasses, for an added touch of elegance and the wow factor.

- Surround the station with finger pastries and fun items, such as S'mores Pops, for a truly exceptional dessert experience.

By featuring buffet stations such as this milkshake bar, you create a total dining experience that will set you apart from the competition.

APPLY YOUR CREATIVITY

This chapter showcased seven special dine-around stations that, in concept and execution, raise the level of quality at a buffet setting. These ideas can be teamed with others similar or be add-ons to other buffet fare of a self-serve nature. The dine-around buffet style makes it possible for the kitchen to combine value, style, flavor, and variety in a simple but elegant manner. An added bonus is that a team of station chefs gets to interact with the guests.

Throughout this chapter—indeed, the entire book—you have been introduced to design concepts intended to change the image that comes to mind for most customers when they hear the word *buffet*. The group of stations in the spotlight here demonstrated how the essentials—good food prepared and displayed in a fresh manner—can become so much more.

A friendly face serves up shakes in all flavors. The key is to offer enough variety to accommodate the labor and/or guest count. For a small intimate buffet of 40 guests, you might offer 4 varieties of shakes; for a banquet of 150, 2 types of shakes would be a better ratio, to ensure quality and keep service time reasonable.

CHAPTER TWELVE

WORKING THE BUFFET

There's an old adage that says you eat first with your eyes. This is true throughout the culinary art world, but perhaps no more so than when speaking of buffets, where food is so openly displayed. When the buffet is well designed and presented, this is a good thing; when it's not, it can have a decidedly negative effect on clients and guests. Reflect on the number of times you have walked up to a buffet and viewed large platters that are two-thirds empty, or opened a chafing dish only to uncover food that clearly has been allowed to sit out a little too long. To ensure that customers are enticed to partake of the offerings on the buffet, it is up to the culinary staff to present and replenish the food so that the buffet is, indeed, a feast for the eyes.

THE BUFFET CANVAS

The buffet canvas is the foundation of all buffets, regardless of type and size. The canvas is many things: It is the table or cart on which all the selections are displayed. It is the platters, the plates, and other serving vessels on which and in which the individual food items in the service area(s) are presented. The canvas also encompasses the decorations used to carry out the theme of the buffet. Even service areas and traffic flow may be considered aspects of the buffet canvas.

Tables and Serving Vessels

You can think of the buffet table or tables as the main area of your canvas. The dishes you create to present on them may be considered your palette of paints. When every dish on the buffet exudes fresh and vibrant colors, a clear indicator of their variety of textures and flavors, your buffet will be inviting, drawing guests directly to it, to sample your artistry.

Recall from Chapter 1 that the tables set up in traditional buffets were covered with cloth and skirting, on which large plates and/or mirrors or silver platters were laid; they were sized to handle the entire volume of the buffet for the duration of the event. Modern buffets take a new approach. The tables are now typically covered with stretch skirting and custom-fitting tops; or finished, colored tables are used, to reflect a design that coordinates with the event. Tables constructed of wood, metal, and other materials, and without coverings or cloths of any kind also are gaining in popularity. Antique tables, too, are enjoying a renaissance in buffet design.

In terms of serving materials, glass, marble, ceramic, and china have replaced the silver platters and mirrors of yesterday's buffets. Smaller plates, as well as platters of various sizes and shapes, are in widespread use; and clay pots and other artisanal ware become focal pieces for pastry.

For food layout in the modern buffet, it's best to take a methodical approach, to ensure consistent production, regardless of the numbers being served. Two other important guidelines are:

- Display the main plate as a complete dish.

- Offer small tastings of pastry on petite plates, rather than whole desserts that become messy and wasteful.

And whether the buffet is designed to serve 50 or 500, the standards should be consistently high, with the primary goal to present fresh food and serve it in a pleasing manner, to all the guests, from first to last.

Color

Many features are added to a buffet for the simple purpose of adding color to the overall display. Without question, color plays a major role in the presentation of food in any venue, but even more so when so on a buffet where there are so many selections to choose from. That said, nothing should ever be added to a dish of any kind *just* for color or to make the overall buffet presentation more attractive. Again, the number-one priority is always the flavor of the food; there must be complete synergy and harmony in the flavor profiles of every dish. When this is achieved, color accents and an inviting presentation tend to happen naturally.

Take, for example, a simple tomato and mozzarella salad. Tomatoes, house-made mozzarella, micro basil, extra-virgin olive oil, and quality vinegar all come together in a mouthwatering and visually inviting dish.

Another good example is a simple but popular item like smoked salmon. A platter laid with thinly sliced, rose-colored salmon, surrounded by decorative serving vessels filled with appropriate accoutrements, is, truly, a picture. The color highlights come from finely minced red onions, the yellow and whites of the eggs, the green capers, and the dark pumpernickel bread and whipped cream cheese. The "portrait" encompasses natural color, flavor harmony, and textural contrast, simply and elegantly drawn.

The colors in this tomato and mozzarella salad are vibrant and natural; the food harmonizes with the texture and flavor contrasts.

THE FLOW OF THE BUFFET

It is important that the individual stations in a buffet layout have a flow that makes sense. In many ways, it is no different from the sequence of selections on an à la carte menu, which lists first plates, salads, soups, main plates, and desserts.

On large buffet tables, it is recommended to arrange the food in a similar order:

- Appetizers
- Salads
- Soup (if it is on the menu)
- Meat platters
- Cheese and dessert displays

A good rule of thumb for the modern buffet is to set up your hot offerings and pastry selections on separate tables. This accomplishes three important objectives. First, it produces a better, more consistent flow of customer traffic. Second, it prevents the heat needed for your hot food away from damaging the cold items. Third, because pastry is the last station on the buffet, you can more easily showcase the artistry of your dessert selections.

For very small buffets that may be restricted to an 8-foot table, follow these guidelines.

- Lay plates and silver on a separate table, to give you enough room to array the food properly.

- Set up the hot items at the very end of the buffet, to keep the heat lamps and burners away from the cold food.

- Place the less-temperature-sensitive foods closer to the heat, and position those foods that must be kept away from heat entirely at the end of the table farthest away from the heat lamps and burners.

When you will be serving larger numbers of guests, double-sided buffets are recommended; or set up separate, duplicate buffets that feature the same items. This will spread out the guests around the room and keep the traffic moving. And, if possible, lay out your plates and any serviceware on a separate table or pick-up point. This way, the buffet space can be utilized 100 percent for the presentation of the food itself. The more small buffet tables you can place at different locations throughout the room, the better the traffic flow will be; and you'll have fewer people waiting in line, meaning that guests will be able to more fully enjoy the experience.

One of the most successful ways to organize a buffet is to first set up what is called the core or foundation buffet table. You then build around the core using smaller buffet tables or action stations. As an exercise, review the menu shown here for a lobster night buffet and then devise a blueprint to show where you would place the core menu items and the supporting items so that you generate not just a smooth flow of traffic, but customer interest and customer excitement, as well.

Another major advantage to this "distribution" system is that customers will approach the buffet as if it were an à la carte menu: They start by selecting salads and first-plate items, go back for their main-plate selections, and return one more time for dessert. For the guest, this assures the dining experience is a civil and relaxed one; for the operation, it minimizes food waste and better enables the culinary team to refresh the buffet stations during the event, to keep it looking fresh.

Lobster Night Buffet Menu

CORE BUFFET ITEMS

These are to be displayed on oval buffet table setup.

House-mixed Greens, Baby Heirloom Tomatoes, Hearts of Palm, Vinaigrette

Clam Chowder or Shrimp Bisque

Baby Shrimp Salad, Avocado, Candied Oranges, Citrus Dressing

THE DETAILS

Butter, cream cheese, jams, jellies,

BUFFET DETAILS

Toaster, tongs, plates, roll up utensils, glasses, serving spoons, risers, small plates

SUPPORTING BUFFET TABLES

Position these tables around the room, within 10 to 12 feet of the core table.

CARVERY STATION

Spiced Flat Iron Steak, Red Wine Sauce

Mashed Potatoes, Roasted Summer Squash

LOBSTER STATION

Boiled or Baked Stuffed Lobster, Drawn Butter, Lemons

Sweet Corn on the Cob

Baked Potatoes

MAIN PLATE STATION

Scottish Salmon Grilled with Olive Oil and Lemon

Roasted Peach Tea Chicken

Pasta Selection of the Evening

PASTRY STATION

Assorted Pastries from the Pastry Kitchen

Boston Crème Pie, Lemon Curd, and Meringue Tarts

Marinated Berries, Honey Biscuits with Chantilly Cream

FRESH SEASONAL FRUIT PIE

Assorted Selection of Ice Cream and Sorbets

Finger Pastries, Brownies, and Lemon Bars

CONSTRUCTING YOUR BUFFET

There are many factors to consider when setting up your buffet: space; time of day; menu; types of tables, serviceware, props, and decorations; client budget; event type or theme; and others. Every buffet is different and should be approached as such. When designing your buffet, it is imperative to balance creativity with sensibility, from the setup of the tables and stations to the layout of food on them. The following tips are provided as food for thought, to help you construct your buffet, regardless of its parameters.

Buffet Design Tips

- Develop schematic templates of all the rooms in which you hold events. For each buffet event, use these templates to sketch the location of your tables and stations for your buffet.

- Take into account the number of people you expect to partake of the buffet, as well as the timeframe for the service. Will the guests arrive for lunch and eat all at the same time? Or is this a two-hour event during which the guests will arrive intermittently?

- Label each table and station to indicate what they will be used for.

- For each table space, sketch roughly what will go on it. Even better, place the menu and equipment needed for that buffet station next to it.

- Identify not only the food you will be serving but also the equipment you will need to prepare it—for example, griddle tops, portable burners, chafers, service tools, platters, and number of plates.

- On buffet action stations, plan for a "back table" where the cook or chef can keep back-up ingredients and tools, such as butter, oil, and spices, and extra pans that may be needed. The action station chef shouldn't have to leave the station to get needed items or stand there unable to prepare the food until a runner brings missing materials.

- Plan for power needs you may have, for lighting and electrical equipment, such as induction grills and warming plates.

- Design effective signage. Make it easy for customers to understand what they're reading. Keep labels short, simple, and clear, and in a style that matches your buffet.

- Staff action buffet stations with trained personnel who can engage with the guests and discuss the food in a succinct but welcoming manner. This type of interaction encourages guests to sample the food being cooked or prepared.

- Where possible, use heat lamps as well as bottom heat from chafers and grill tops or burners. This adds to the light dimension and also keeps hot food hot much more efficiently.

- Choose plate size carefully. Stay away from too large a plate, which guests will tend to overload, producing food waste. Good plate-size guidelines are as follows: for a reception, 7 to 8 inches; for a full lunch or dinner, 10 inches; for pastry, 7 inches.

- Offer a variety of salad dressings and condiments on the side. This gives customers a choice and keeps salad greens looking and tasting fresh. That said, if the buffet is one where guests will break from a meeting and get up all at the same time to eat, then tossing and dressing the greens is acceptable. A good practice is to toss your salad greens with a very light vinaigrette or olive oil and display the dressing on the side.

- For barbeque or outdoor buffets, or for casual events that feature steaks, burgers, French fries, and the like, it's advisable to place the condiments on a separate table. This accomplishes two things: The guests will not tie up the buffet line choosing and putting on condiments, and it will keep the buffet tidier.

With those tips in mind, take a close look at the following photos of some buffet displays, to understand why they work. On this buffet service, the small plates and tomato salad are ideal accompaniments to the hot selections.

This very elegant lunch or dinner buffet demonstrates the canvas techniques at work. Height used in concert with small plates and smaller platters results in a customer-friendly buffet that is inviting, and stays fresh.

SERVICE AREAS

The service areas, too, are part of the larger buffet canvas. Their layout, like all other elements of the buffet, should be simple—from color to shapes to height and to flow. Again, the canvas is the foundation on which you will lay your food and service vessels.

Set up empty trays and displays on your table prior to the start of the event. This will help you to make appropriate adjustments, as necessary, to create the best flow for the buffet. Doing this also makes it easier to take into account color, shapes, and height of both the display pieces and the food that will be placed on them.

It's important to view the buffet from all angles, to see it as the guests will. Based on what you observe, make the appropriate adjustments to the display to show off the food to its best effect.

ICE CARVING

Traditionally, sculptures of many types have been used as the centerpieces for grand buffets as a way to dazzle the guest and accentuate the event or holiday at hand. Of those, ice carvings/sculptures are among the most popular.

Ice carving, as its name implies, uses ice as the raw material. Sculptures carved from ice may be abstract, realistic, three-dimensional, or in a form of art that directly reflects the event; and they may be functional or purely decorative.

Generally, sculptures are carved from blocks of ice that are carefully selected to fit the sculptor's purposes; most importantly, they should be free of undesired impurities and cracks. Typically, ideal carving blocks are made from pure, clean filtered water. However, very clear and transparent ice is dependent on the freezing process as well, not just the purity of the water.

Clear ice blocks are usually produced by slow freezing from one direction, often with circulation of the water to allow any impurities to escape. Certain machines and processes allow for slow freezing and the removal of impurities; they are able to produce the clear blocks of ice favored by ice carvers. One of the most preferred types of ice for carving/sculpting is blue ice.

The temperature of the working environment obviously will affect how quickly a piece must be completed before suffering the deleterious effects of melting. Many ice carvers sculpt the foundation for their pieces in a freezer or just outside the freezer area and then finish the details inside the freezer. The life of an ice sculpture is determined primarily by the temperature of its display environment, in conjunction with its size. An ice sculpture, on average, will last from three to six or more hours.

In the past, ice sculptors used razor-sharp chisels and handsaws specifically designed for cutting and shaping ice. Today, new technologies have given ice artists more and more exacting tools to work with. Chain saws, power saws, routers, and other equipment make it possible to produce more precise and highly detailed ice creations. In addition, logos and other fine detail work can be produced to very exacting levels of precision using computers and lasers.

Computer numerical control (CNC) machines and molding systems, though costly, are being used more often today to create sculptures and complicated logos from ice that could not be reproduced by even the most talented carver working by hand.

Here, Chef Joseph Albertelli, the chef gardé who carved the ice in the photos that appear in this section, shares his insights about ice carving.

Chef Joe's 10 Guidelines for Ice Carving

1. *Safety.* Ice blocks and sculptures are very heavy, and the tools used to carve them potentially dangerous, so safety must be the number-one priority when dealing with ice, from production to presentation on the buffet table.

2. *Mise en place.* Having everything in order is every bit as important in ice carving as it is in cooking. This is true for reasons of safety, execution, and display. A chef/sculptor must have the time to create templates, the proper conditions in which to execute a carving, and adequate and appropriate space to store the sculpture; finally, an appropriate place must be available to display the work safely and to its best effect, even in the middle of a busy reception where several things are going on at once. With a good game plan you can accomplish a lot more than you think you can.

3. *The right ice block.* When choosing the ice for a sculpture, make sure the block is free of impurities, which can show up in the final sculpture, causing it to look unfinished or unprofessional.

4. *Cutting or purchasing.* There are advantages to both cutting your own ice and purchasing it from a supplier. If you choose to cut the ice yourself, once you obtain a basic toolkit, producing the sculptures becomes less expensive. Cutting your own ice also enables you to add another skill to your arsenal. If, on the other hand, you decide to purchase ice from a supplier, it will be less time-consuming, and you will be helping to support your local ice shop.

5. *Strong lines.* This refers to the silhouette of the sculpture—its outline. Strong lines also provide a visual path from one point to another, to help express a sculpture's movement.

6. *Geometric form and shape.* These are important for giving a sculpture its dimension and depth.

7. *Proper proportion.* Proportion shows how different areas of the ice sculpture relate to one another in comparison to size, and give the sculpture a more realistic look.

8. *Detail.* Keep in mind that details last about three hours in an ice sculpture and so will be lost if the previous areas have not been adequately addressed. Details made with a chisel or die grinder can produce a prism effect in the ice, adding character, texture, and a finished look to the sculpture.

9. *Overall impression.* This is, essentially, a statement about the sculpture as a whole, and takes proportion, uniformity, and detail into consideration.

10. *Display.* When displaying an ice sculpture, several factors come into play:

- Tempering
- Transporting
- Lifting
- Drainage
- Lighting

When taking a sculpture out of the freezer for display it is important to temper it to a clear state. If this step is not taken, the sculpture might crack, due to extreme temperature change. Know ahead of time where the sculpture will be displayed so you can plan how to move the piece from point A to B. Once you get the sculpture to the display area, lifting the piece is the next step. Sculptures can weigh several hundred pounds, so it is best to use a lift to safely hoist it into position. Lifts cost a couple hundred dollars, but are worth every cent.

CHEF ALBERTELLI DESCRIBES THE DISPLAY PROCESS IN GREATER DETAIL:

I can place a 200-pound sculpture on a buffet by myself. I cut a piece of ETHAFOAM™ and put it in the drip pan so that once the lift reaches the pan, the sculpture slides right on top of the foam in the pan; then crushed ice is added.

Make sure to leave enough room for the water to properly drain. Place a five-gallon bucket under the table and run a tube from the pan to the bucket. The tube can be hidden with excess tablecloth and table skirting so it is not visible to the guests. Then light the sculpture to highlight your finished work of art.

The buffet has undergone a great deal of change over time, yet it remains as popular as ever with even the most discriminating guests today. By "working the buffet" as described in this chapter, you will exceed guest expectations and offer a unique dining experience, one that is fun yet elegant, offers something for everyone, and, last but not least, showcases your operation and the talent of your culinary team.

No longer is the buffet just a vehicle for volume food service; it is an opportunity to offer a dining experience unlike any other. By paying careful attention to all the areas of your buffet canvas—analyzing your buffet blueprint, planned service style, and menu—you will achieve winning results.

CHAPTER THIRTEEN

MENUS: CONCEPTS AND ACCENTUATING IDEAS

Raising the bar, meeting new customer demands, and maintaining the excitement in buffets are challenges for operators everywhere. By now, however, you have seen that, by enhancing old favorites, taking a different approach, or developing an entirely new concept, you can change longstanding—and sometimes negative—perceptions of buffet food.

You've also read about the importance of producing in modern buffets what I call the "wow factor" in all areas, from the style, the design, and the flow to the way the food is prepared, displayed, and served. All are essential ingredients to ensuring a successful modern buffet dining experience. What do I mean by the "wow factor"? Simply this: When you stand back and review the buffet you have created, do you say "wow"? If it says wow to you, it will to the guest, too.

Getting to wow starts with an idea or concept, a menu, and a plan. Once you have those, you are on your way to buffet success. This chapter is intended to help you accomplish that, by presenting a selection of menus, ideas, and concepts. It's also intended to get your creative juices flowing, to encourage you to brainstorm with others, and to lay a solid foundation on which you can build and execute your ideas.

Before getting to the menus and concepts, let's review a few important facts about modern buffets:

- Buffets have wide customer acceptance.

- Properly managed, buffets can help you save on labor and food costs.

- Buffets bring all departments together to work as a team, generating enthusiasm, instilling pride, and building morale.

- Once the foundation and standards for a buffet have been established, through creativity, and by fine-tuning, you can create a "wow" repertoire.

- Revising and updating old favorites and traditional ideas can lead to the creation of stellar new concepts and menu ideas.

- Today's buffet menus should offer diversity, add excitement to your foodservice operation, and produce the wow factor for your guests.

Buffet Menus That Wow

Developing a menu is the first stage in planning for any buffet. It is the basis for everything else to come. You'll use it as a marketing tool and selling point for clients—it's a tangible you can use to help convince them to book a function at your venue. It will also be a major factor when you set up your buffet, from the layout to the design to the décor, even to the service tools you'll need to accomplish the presentation. And, of course, you'll use the menu to order your food. From start to finish, then, the menu is the most important document in executing a successful buffet, one that exceeds all expectations.

Most operations have a collection of house menus they use as standards, from which the customers can choose and then customize for their specific purpose. Many menus list a selection of items, ranging from à la carte to complete buffet selections. Buffet menus typically have themes. A "Nineteenth-Hole Luncheon Buffet," for example, could be used to market lunch at a country club, golf club, or a resort with golf courses. Others capture the spirit and essence of their locale. A hotel in Washington, DC, for example, might feature menu specials such as a congressional reception, a Senate power breakfast buffet, and so on. Many buffet menus are, not surprisingly, themed for holiday events, such as a Christmas tree lighting, a children's Halloween party, a New Year's celebration, to name a few. The buffet menu may also be driven by the customer's wishes, such as a family that requests a dine-around wedding buffet rather than the traditional seated dinner, or a company that wants a BBQ theme buffet for its annual meeting. As I've said many times throughout this book, the possibilities are endless, limited only by your creativity.

That said, it's absolutely imperative to write a menu that you and your team can produce. Promising too much and then failing to deliver is a direct road to failure. Use the following tips to guide you as you take this first, crucial step to ensure the success of your buffet.

Tips for Successful Menu Writing

- *Offer variety.* Give your customers not only a variety of food options but also price points and types of buffet service.

- *Provide à la carte or "upsell" options on your buffet menu.* A seafood station or adult milkshake bar can go a long way to enhancing a standard buffet.

- *Sell buffet stations à la carte even for sit-down dinner events.* For example, for a wedding, offer the couple a "Bride and Groom's Celebration of Pastries," rather than the standard plated dessert choices of various finger pastries. And serve desserts in a separate room, where guests can enjoy them at their leisure. This allows for more social interaction, and guests can choose not only what they would like to eat, but how much and when.

- *Describe menu items in clear, easy-to-understand language.* That does not mean you can't also use words that entice and excite. A well-written menu will have the guest saying, "Wow! I am hungry just thinking about the food on this buffet."

- *Know your limitations.* There is no sense in featuring a buffet menu from a five-star property if your operation does not have five-start talent to produce it, along with the necessary equipment and all the other means required to properly execute the buffet.

- *Be honest.* You've heard the phrase "truth in advertising"; it applies to menus, as well. Misleading customers can cost you business. If your breakfast buffet menu says "fresh-squeezed orange and grapefruit juice," then that is what the customer will expect, and what they are paying for. Do not write "fresh-squeezed" if you are serving carton juice—regardless of how good it is. Do not write "oven-roasted turkey breast" if you purchase and use a commercial brand of turkey breast such as that sold in most deli operations. "Oven-roasted" implies *real* turkey breast; not pressed and shaped to look like turkey.

- *Use adjectives judiciously.* "Jumbo shrimp," for example, may mean different things to different people. "Jumbo" usually implies that those shrimp will be huge; if they are not, you will disappoint the client and the guests. Keep in mind, the customer will always perceive things bigger and better. Likewise, "fresh" means fresh, not out of a can or jar.

- *Create synergy.* Include selections on your buffet menus whose products synergize with those on other menus in the operation. This will help you to plan your inventory efficiently and better manage your food costs.

- *Leave room for flexibility.* Describe items as "seasonal" or "a selection of…." Don't commit, for example, to serving raspberries and blueberries year-round, as those fruits double or triple in price at certain times of the year. It's much more cost-effective to offer seasonal fruit and berries. Similarly, offer other seasonal or market choices on your buffet menus. For example: Pan-Roasted Swordfish with Tomato and Artichoke Salsa (Spiced Peach Salsa available June to August).

- *Include side dishes that harmonize with the protein of main-plate items.* Feature accoutrements that add up to a complete package of buffet offerings and that give good value to the customer. A carvery station should, for example, include a sauce, relish, or chutney; a type of bread or roll that suits the main item; and perhaps a salad, starch, or vegetable.

- *Balance your menu selections.* Offer seafood, a variety of meats, vegetarian options, classics, old favorites, modern concepts, chocolate, fruits, and more. In short, have something for everyone.

- *Know your audience.* A holiday buffet event at a club or hotel, for example, is sure to bring in a large number of children, so it may make sense to set up a separate buffet serving a child-friendly menu. Doing this will please not only the children but their parents as well, who then won't have to worry what to feed their picky eaters.

- *Focus on the details.* It's the little things that can take a basic, popular menu item and lift it to another level. For example, accompany a traditional Caesar salad with parmesan cracklings and warm grape tomatoes.

- *Highlight specialty items.* Use a different font, or boldface, to draw guests' attention to a signature item or special treat on your menu.

- *Do not hesitate to use the chef's or cook's name on an item.* Personalizing an item gives the team member a sense of pride, which will carry over in his or her work and be evident to guests. It also adds a personal touch that guests will appreciate when they approach a station.

Sample Menus

On the pages that follow, you'll see a sample of menus written for various events that were very successful from both a customer and venue viewpoint. Remember, menus are strong selling points. Never underestimate the power of a menu to excite and tempt the client and, ultimately, the guest.

 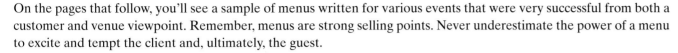

Wine Dinner Buffet

SELECTION OF COLD OFFERINGS FROM THE GARDE MANGER

Mixed Greens with Mango Vinaigrette, Boston Bibb with Ranch Dressing and Pork Cracklings

Lump Crab and Avocado with Chardonnay Vinaigrette

House-made Mozzarella Terrine with Port Wine Reduction and Candied Tomatoes

Foie Gras Torchon with Cherry Compote

House-baked Croissants and Brioche Rolls

GUEST CHEF OF THE EVENING

Salmon Mignons, Braised Sauerkraut, Potatoes in Mustard Sauce

Roasted Shrimp, Crispy Bacon Belly, and Olive Oil Mashed potato

Shoulder of Lamb Confit, Spinach and Feta Ravioli, Lamb Jus

Bibb Lettuce, Red Onion Salad

Beef Short Rib Sandwich

Pickled Vegetables and Sweet Mustard

Roasted Cod, Chili-glazed Bacon Belly, and Truffle Risotto

Mushroom and Tarragon Cream Soup

Slow-roasted Pork, Chorizo, Tomato and Pepper Sofrito, Tostones, and Avocado Salad

EGGPLANT PIROGUE LOUIS

Stew of Crawfish, Shrimp with Eggplant

Braised Veal Shank, Mirepoix of Chestnuts and Root Vegetables, Creamy Polenta

Warm Apple Fritters, Vanilla Bean Ice Cream, Calvados Sauce

Grilled Lemon Curd Pound Cake, Blueberry Ice Cream, Dried Blueberry Crumble

At this event, eight wineries set up tables for wine tasting. Six other elegant buffet stations were attended by guest chefs who were bought in to make the event a bit more special. It also gave the culinary team an opportunity to work with other chefs of a star caliber. The station features the chefs who personally prepared guests' tasting selections.

Irish Night

Buffet of Traditional Irish and American Irish Dishes

ON THE TABLE

Bread Basket of Strawberry Scones, Irish Soda Bread, Irish Butter

STARTERS

House Salad of Lettuces, Pickled Cabbage, Potato Croutons, Irish Bacon, Carrot Whisky Dressing

Rocket and Baby Spinach with Chickpeas, Irish Soda Bread Croutons and Roasted Cherry Tomatoes, with Red Wine Vinaigrette

Oak-smoked Irish Salmon, Baby Capers, Caramelized Onions, and Chive Sour Cream

Chicken Liver Terrine, Wild Blackcurrant, and Chili Relish

MAIN PLATES

Irish Lamb Stew

Corned Beef and Cabbage

Skirt Steak with Guinness

Chicken Breast Casserole in a Creamy Smoked Bacon and Leek Sauce, Mashed Potato

Roast Carrots and Parsnips Roasted in Honey and Thyme

Gallagher's Own Thick-cut Chips

PASTRY

Traditional Apple Sponge with Bailey's Irish Cream

Baked Fruits and Irish Mist Egg Custard

Wild Berry Mousse with Short Crust Biscuit

Ethnic-themed buffets can be very successful, as long as you do the research to ensure that your menu accurately reflects the cuisine. That said, some adjustment and interpretations in the food may be needed, as truly authentic dishes may not be what your customer expects or wants.

Clam Bake

RECEPTION

Clams and Oysters on the Half Shell, Shrimp Cocktail, Crab Claws

Mignonette Sauce, Citron Cocktail Sauce, Lemons, Limes, Fresh-grated Horseradish and Chipotle Tabasco

PEI Mussels Steamed with Dark Beer Garlic and Herbs

Mini New York-Style Ruebens

California Rolls, Spicy Tuna Rolls, Spider Rolls, and Shrimp Tempura Rolls

Pickled Ginger, Fresh Wasabi, and Soy Sauce

Baked Stuffed Clams, Brioche Apple Bacon Stuffing with Clams, and Candied Garlic

Not Your Dad's Franks in a Blanket (Mini Frankfurters Baked in Phyllo Dough with Stone-ground Mustard and Sauerkraut)

DINE-AROUND DINNER

New England Clam Chowder with Oyster Crackers

Iceberg Wedges with Thousand Island Dressing, Red Onion Brûlée, and Warm Bacon Bits

Grilled Summer Vegetables, Balsamic Glaze, Extra-Virgin Olive Oil

Caesar Salad with Oven-roasted Grape Tomatoes

Selection of Summer Tomatoes, House-made Mozzarella, Pesto Dressing

Pressed Melon with Mâche and Goat Cheese

Roasted and Crispy Asparagus with Truffle Vinaigrette

SMOKING BBQ STATION

House-smoked Brisket of Beef with Chipotle BBQ Sauce

Peach Tea Smoked Chicken Wraps with Peach Tea BBQ Sauce

Root Beer BBQ Ribs and Vinegar Pulled Pork

Selection of BBQ Sauces, Potato Rolls, Honey Butter Corn Bread, Coleslaw

---

LOBSTER STATION

Boiled Maine Lobster, Drawn Butter, Wrapped Lemon Halves

Sweet Corn on the Cob, Yukon Gold Baked Potatoes

DESSERT BAR

Fresh Strawberry Shortcake

Marinated Strawberries, Strawberry Ice Cream, Whipped Cream, Dried Strawberry Flakes on Sponge Cake Rounds

Assorted Brownies, Pecan Turtles, Fudge, S'mores, and Grand Marnier

Mini Cheesecakes, Coconut Macaroons

Ice Cream Sundae Bar

Vanilla and Chocolate Ice Cream

Godiva Fudge Sauce, Carmel Sauce, Spiced Pecans, Candied Walnuts, Bing Cherries, Fresh Cream

---

Who doesn't love a clam bake? Fun reception food kicks off a fun evening!

Family Fun Night Buffet

FUN STATION FOR THE KIDS

Corn Dogs on a Stick

English Muffin Pizza

Crispy Macaroni and Cheese Balls

Pretzel Bites, Chicken Tenders, French Fries

FROM THE GRILL

Display of Offerings

Assorted Kabobs: Burgers, Chicken Breast, Fresh Catch of the Day, All-beef Hot Dogs, Sirloin Steak, BBQ Ribs, Peach Tea Chicken, Cast-iron-Baked Beans

BUILD YOUR OWN PASTA

Choice of Ravioli, Fusilli, Penne

Sauces: Pomodoro, Vodka, Meat, Pesto

Toppings: Baby Shrimp, Seasonal Vegetables, Chicken, Sausage, Grated Cheese

BUILD YOUR OWN CHEF'S SALAD

Assorted Greens, Baby Iceberg, Romaine

Olives, Tomatoes, Feta Cheese, Aged Cheddar, Red Onion, Cucumbers

Grilled Vegetables, Croutons, Roasted Turkey, French Ham, Baby Shrimp, Tuna in Olive Oil, Roasted Peppers, Artichokes, Eggs, Bacon

Caesar, Balsamic, Ranch, Thousand Island, Olive Oil and Vinegar

FROM THE BUFFET AND CHAFERS

Soup of the Evening, Assorted Bread and Rolls, Butter

House-smoked Salmon and Accoutrements

Chicken Marsala

Rice Pilaf

Salmon Medallions with Braised Sauerkraut and Mustard Sauce

Crispy Pork Chops, Apple Sauce

Glazed Seasonal Vegetables

Chef's Selection of the Evening

FROM THE PASTRY SHOPPE

Fresh Frozen Fruit Squeeze Cups

Banana Split Bar

Scooped-to-Order Vanilla, Chocolate, and Strawberry Ice Cream

Chocolate Fountain, with Pound Cake Squares, Assorted Fresh Fruit, and Marshmallows

Small Bites: Brownies, Carrot Cake Bars, Chocolate Chip Cookies, Snickerdoodles, and Oatmeal Raisin Cookies

Mom's Icebox Cake, Tiramisu

Carved Melon Baskets with Fresh Fruit

Cheesecakes: Caramel Pecan Turtle, Fresh Strawberry, Godiva Chocolate

With the focus of many these days on family dining, even banquet events get into the spirit, especially when families are part of the guest list. Do not be surprised at how many adults hit the kids' buffet, as well, so be prepared.

Buffet Dining with Fun and Style

CHEF'S TAPAS DISPLAY

Serrano Ham with Sweet Melon

Seared Cod with Olive Oil Mashed Potato

Scallops, Ceviche-style

Red Pepper and Goat Cheese Terrine

Roasted Mushrooms and Truffles

Olive Oil Tomatoes with Basil

Fresh-shucked Clams with Chipolata Pesto

CHEF'S ACTION STATIONS

New England Lobster Rolls

Summer Peking Duck Wraps

Crab Cakes with Sweet Corn Relish

Shrimp with Clam and Potato Sauce

Adobe-braised Short Ribs with Vegetable Risotto

CARVERY STATION

Rack of Lamb, Rosemary Spoon Bread, Garlic and Tomato
Mint Jam

PASTRY STATION

English Trifle in Martini Glasses

Warm Double-Chocolate Pound Cake, Roasted Peaches,
Carmel Ice Cream, Sea Salt

Assorted Finger Pastries, Individual Summer Fruit Pies,
House-made Chocolate Truffles

This simple but fun food buffet was provided to guests after two days of meetings and seminars. At the buffet stations guests were able to network in a more relaxed atmosphere while they enjoyed a wide variety of food choices. The quality of food and service was equal to that of a formal sit-down dinner.

Lunch Buffet

French Beans, Olive Oil Poached Artichoke Bottoms, Tomatoes, Endive and Pancetta Ranch Dressing

Signature Greek Salad: Butter Lettuce, Endive, Cucumber, Olives, Imported Feta, Roasted Tomatoes, and Red Wine Oregano Dressing

Hearts of Romaine Filled with Shitake and Queso Blanco Cheese, Avocado, Oven-dried Tomatoes, Olives, Chipotle Dressing

Olive Oil Poached Chicken

Roasted Wild Mushrooms, Tarragon, Parma Ham and Asparagus, Olive Aioli

Veal Milanese; Breaded Veal Cutlet Pan Fried, with a Salad of Arugula, Variety of Olive Oil Tomatoes, and Balsamic Cream

Petite Filet Mignon, Olive Oil Mashed Potato, Seasonal Vegetables, Beef Jus Lié, Merlot Syrup

Sea Bass, Roasted In Olive Oil, Potato Parisienne with Vegetable Fricassee

Roasted Vegetable Risotto, Carrot Ginger Jus, Aged Parmigiano

PASTRY

Meringue Napoleon with Trio of Sorbets and Raspberry Purée

Individual Chocolate Boston Cream Pie with Strawberries

Apple Pear Strudel Dusted with Confectioner's Sugar, Caramel Whipped Cream

A simple lunch buffet with menu offerings that ensure variety for all guests, plenty of vegetarian options, and great classic desserts.

Buffet Dinners

CELEBRATION OF AMERICA DINNER BUFFET

House-baked Rolls and Breads

Seasonal Fruit Salad with Mint

French Bean Salad with Pecans and Artichokes

Iceberg Wedges with Creamy Bacon Dressing

Grilled Club Steak of Natural Beef with Demi Glace Butter

Pan-seared Fillet of Snapper or Sea Bass with Thyme Honey Sauce

Oven-fried Breast of Chicken

Buttermilk Mashed Potatoes

Baby Carrots with Bourbon Glaze

Sautéed Spinach

PASTRY

Warm Chocolate Bread Pudding with Vanilla Sauce

German Chocolate Cake

Signature Macaroons

A themed buffet dinner that features comfort American food with elegance.

HOLIDAY BUFFET MENUS

Holidays are truly special occasions; for many, they mark the few times during a year that family members and friends come together to enjoy each other's company and the day. At the center of these celebrations is food, whether shared at home, a restaurant, a club, or a hotel. I tell my chefs it is our job to make each holiday a fond memory for our guests by providing a dining experience that is second to none.

 ## Easter Dine-Around

EASTER SELECTIONS FROM THE CHEF'S GARDE KITCHEN

Smoked Pastrami Salmon, Maple-cured Salmon, and Lox, with all the accoutrements plus Mini Bagels and Pumpernickel

Spring Harvest Salad

Baby Zucchini, Snap Peas, Radishes, Broccolini, Gold Beets, Asparagus, Shaved Manchego, Ice Wine Dressing

Poached Prawns and Oysters with Chipotle Cocktail Sauce, and Yuzu Pepper Mignonette

MARKET PLATTERS

Cured Meats, Cheese, Prosciutto with Melon, Ham, Baguettes

INSALATA

Arugula and Mesclun, Lemon-poached Pear, Toasted Hazelnuts, Gorgonzola

Butter Lettuce

Avocado, Point Reyes Blue Cheese, Champagne-Herb Vinaigrette

Organic Asparagus

Poached Egg, Warm Bacon Vinaigrette

Grilled Chicken Paillard

Barley, Artichokes, Arugula Salad, Olive Dressing

Red Salad Beets, Red Leaves, Roasted Peppers, Raspberries, and Goat Cheese

Roasted Vegetable Salad

Portobello Mushrooms, Mozzarella, Basil, Olive Tapenade

Grilled Pacific Salmon

Watercress Salad, Sweet Red Onion Dressing, Dill Crème

Green Salad

Iceberg and Romaine Salad, Yellow and Red Tomatoes, Green Goddess Dressing

Fennel and Orange Salad

Olive Oil Poached Scallops, Limoncello Vinaigrette

This is a diverse buffet menu used to feed almost one thousand people over a five-hour period. The ability to use small plates, platters, and chef-attended stations ensures fresh food and flavor presentations from beginning to end.

Parade of Chefs Easter Dine-Around

BRUNCH FARE

Berkshire Bacon, Breakfast Sausage, Red Bliss Morning Potatoes

Assorted Pastries, Hot Cross Buns

Omelets from Free-range Eggs

Selection of Spinach, Mushrooms, Caramelized Onions, Cheese, and Ham

SIGNATURE HOLIDAY FARE

Hand-carved Roasted Leg of Lamb, Garlic and Mint

Lamb Osso Bucco

Ratatouille/Rice Pilaf

Lamb Jus, House-made Mint Jelly

ITALIAN EASTER

Our Specialty Traditional "Lasagna Bolognese"

Ravioli with Roasted Eggplant, Red Peppers, and Mozzarella

Ravioli with Sausage and Broccoli Rabe

Petite Rigatoni with Butter Sauce

Grandma Civatello's Napolitano Meat Pie

FROM THE SEA

Snapper with Wilted Spinach Salad

Stuffed Flounder with Lobster Sauce

CASUAL FAMILY FARE

Petite Club Steaks and Roasted Potatoes

Hamburger Quesadilla

Almond-crusted Chicken

Macaroni and Cheese

EASTER CARVERY

Roast Prime Rib of Beef, Jus Lié, Horseradish Sauce

Roasted Easter Ham, Maple Pineapple Sauce

Assorted Rolls

SOMETHING SPECIAL

Real Italian Porchetta, Ciabatta Rolls, Garlic Mayonnaise

Easter Pastry Display

Easter Bunny Cupcakes

Zeppole

Bunny Carrot Cookies

Assorted Thumbprint Cookies

Our Signature Easter Ricotta Pies and Noodle Pies

Lemon Tarts, Chocolate Mousse Cakes

Filled Chocolate Biscuits

Easter Flower Boxes with Cake, Cookie, and Candy Lollipops

Assorted Fruit Mousse in Egg Cups

Ice Cream Bar

Sorbet Bar

Easter Candies

Thanksgiving Buffet

Display of House-made Terrines and Ham

Apples and Poached Pears

Seafood Display: Roasted, Cured, and Smoked Seafood
(Salmon, Trout, Tuna, Shrimp) with Mustard Dill Sauce,
Horseradish Cream

Gourmet Cheese Display with Crostini and Crusted Bread

Steamed and Crispy Vegetable Display in Carved Pumpkin
Bowls

Creamy and Ginger Dip

Maple Syrup-baked Sweet Onion

Roasted Fall Squash Salad

Black-Eyed Pea Salad

Marinated Green Asparagus

Spiced Roasted Pear with Chestnut Purée

Creamer Potato and Cucumber Salad

Celery Root, Apple, and Walnut Salad

Caesar Salad and Mixed Green Salad

Selection of Three Dressings

Roasted Pumpkin Soup with Butter-poached Lobster,
Candied Vanilla Pumpkin Seeds

Carved New England Free-range Roasted Turkey with
Traditional Turkey Gravy

Herb and Mustard Spiced Strip Loin of Beef, Beef Jus Lié

Roasted Halibut Fillet with Creamed Savoy Cabbage

Confit of Turkey Legs and Thighs

Orange Cranberry Relish, Red Onion Chutney

Traditional Stuffing

Candied Sweet Potato with Marshmallow Crust

Traditional Mashed Potato

Herb and Bacon Grits

Green Beans with Herbs and Apple Cider Glazed Carrots

Sautéed Cipollinis with Maple Butter

FROM THE PASTRY SHOPPE

Freshly Sliced Fruit

Poached and Marinated Fruits in Martini Glasses

Pecan Pie, Pumpkin Pie with Fresh Cream, Deep-dish Apple
Pie, Crumb Cherry Pie

Pumpkin Cheesecake, Creamy New York Cheesecake

Pumpkin Roulade with Ginger Cream and Candied Ginger

Thanksgiving Ice Cream Bar: Apple Cobbler, Vanilla Bean,
Chocolate, Pumpkin, and Butter Pecan Ice Creams

Assorted Cookies and Cupcakes

A bountiful buffet of seasonal flavors and favorites presented in a modern way.

Christmas Eve Candlelight Dinner Buffet

HOT AND COLD ANTIPASTI BAR

Serrano Ham with Pressed Melon

Roasted Trio of Sweet Peppers with Garlic Vinaigrette

Roman-style Artichokes

Asparagus with Shaved Pecorino, Truffle Vinaigrette

Baby Iceberg Wedges, Eggnog Ranch Dressing

Gift-wrapped Romaine Hearts, Thousand Island Dressing

Roasted Red and Yellow Tomatoes, Frantoia Oil, Aged Balsamic Vinegar

Avocado, Citrus Salad

Baccala Salad, Grilled Calamari Salad

Imported Meat and Cheese Selection

Endive, Goat Cheese, and Raspberry Salad

Stuffed Peppers with Eggplant Caponata

Stuffed Mushrooms

Eggplant Rollatini

Fried Mozzarella, Sauce Pomodoro

NIGHT OF THE SEVEN FISHES

Poached Shrimp, Candied Lemon Cocktail Sauce

Poached and Smoked, Decorated Salmon

Assorted Shellfish Roasted with Tomatoes and Garlic

Sea Bass Sicilian Style

Shrimp Francese

Fried Calamari, Cherry Pepper Sauce

Sole Florentine

SANTA'S CHEFS COOKING

Hand-rolled Sushi Station

Chicken Piquant with Rice

Lobster Ravioli, Lobster Jus and Butter Sauce

Stuffed Shells, Nonna's Meatballs

Gumbo

Roast Leg of Lamb, Basil Lamb Jus, Confit of Lamb Shoulder, Fondant Potatoes

CARVERY

Chef Leonard's Signature Item

Classic Turducken with Pan Gravy

Roast Sirloin of Brandt Natural Beef, Jus

Mashed Potatoes, Glazed Root Vegetables

CHEFS COOKING FOR THE KIDS CHRISTMAS EVE BUFFET

Macaroni and Cheese

Roasted Petite Chicken Breast, Apple Carrots

Rudolph the Red-Nosed Baked Potato

Little Fish and Chips

North Pole Mini Meatballs

Iceberg and Fruit Salad

SIGNATURE PASTRY BUFFET

Holiday Croque en Bouche

Edible Ornament Christmas Tree

Holiday Chocolates, Candies, and Cookies

Tis the Season Ice Cream Bar

Bûche de Noël

Classic Black Forest Cake

Petite Pumpkin, Eggnog, and Vanilla Cheesecakes

Snowball Cupcakes

Icebox Cake

A buffet like no other, designed to feature a menu with something for everyone, from the antipasti bar to the night of the seven fishes, to chef-attended buffet stations to a stunning pastry buffet.

BUFFET CONCEPTS

Chefs, venue managers, and food and beverage professionals are on a never-ending search to find something imaginative to do to raise the bar at the modern buffet, which owes its energy to new concepts and innovative ways of presentation. But before they can advance their craft successfully, they must first have an understanding of the past, of the history of buffet-style dining.

The buffets of yesteryear all shared a common goal: to be grand, to make a statement, to impress. This was achieved by designing opulent presentations and serving large portions of food from large service vessels, all arrayed on one very large grouping of tables, which were almost always situated in the center of the room. From soup to nuts, it was all there in one expansive display. The concept behind these grand buffets was pretty uniform and usually based on an event, an occasion, or a holiday. Those days are gone.

Modern buffet concepts are developed to build and enhance business, to top the competitor, and to be creative and different and give the customer variety. This is especially true at operations and venues with less transient business, such as clubs. Buffet concepts are also developed to meet market demands and provide diverse customer experiences. No matter what the buffet concept, however, the keys for success are the same. They are:

- Know your market before launching any concept.

- Develop a concept plan. Ideally, this should be a file containing the menu, an order sheet, and a setup blueprint or digital picture of the layout for reference, to ensure consistency, identify signature recipes, dictate storage directions for all décor items, and so on.

- Create an attractive presentation that both meets the concept objectives and showcases the talent of the culinary staff.

- Set up a variety of independent stations to compose your buffet, rather than one large table on which all the items on the menu are laid out.

- Serve high-quality, fresh, delicious food in a simple but elegant manner.

- Prepare a reasonable menu selection, one that will please today's demanding and diverse consumer base.

- Personalize buffet stations with friendly staff; or set them up as stand-alone self-serve stations.

- Let the cuisine and presentations speak for themselves. Don't overuse decorations or props; your concept should be apparent from your food display.

SPECIALTY MEETING BREAK CONCEPTS

Take Me Out to the Ball Game Fun

Bring the ball game to your customers with a fun and flavorful break-out session.

Freshly Popped Popcorn

Warm Pretzels with Mustard

Candy Bars, Cracker Jacks

Ball Park Hot Dogs, Relish, Mustard, and Sauerkraut

Assorted Ice Cream Bars

Assorted Soft Drinks and Spring Waters

The Energy Break

For those breaks where a quick pick-me-up is needed.

Whole Fresh Fruits, Sliced Seasonal Fruits

Granola Bars, Trail Mix, Assorted Nuts

Zucchini-Walnut Bread

Assorted Soft Drinks and Spring Waters

Freshly Brewed Coffee and Select Teas

English Tea Break

Traditional English afternoon tea makes any meeting break elegant.

Assorted Tea Sandwiches: Smoked Salmon, Roast Beef and Watercress, Cucumber and Cream Cheese, Egg and Pickled Onion, Olive Oil Tuna and Caper Mayonnaise

Tea Pastries and Cookies: Petite Fruit Tarts, Pecan Diamonds, Macaroons, Napoleon Shortbread, Biscuits with Jam and Crème Fraîche

Assorted Signature Teas, Cream, Honey, Raw Sugar, and Lemon

Set up these meeting break buffet styles with harmonizing props, priced per person.

INDIVIDUAL STATION CONCEPTS

Below are some individual station concepts that can be added on to standard buffets or teamed together for a unique tasting of offerings.

House of Noodles

Udon Noodles

Shredded Roasted Chicken

Pulled Spiced Beef

Baby Shrimp

Wok-fried Vegetables

Petite Tempura of Shrimp and Vegetables

Choice of Beef, Chicken, or Vegetable Broth

For this station, make udon noodles with hot, slightly thickened broth. Serve in a tall bowl or Asian takeout boxes; provide toppings and chopsticks.

The Chef's Lollipop Bar

Melon and Prosciutto

Fig and Serrano Ham

Strawberry and Ricotta Mousse

Grilled Pineapple and Sage

Smoked Salmon and Cream Cheese

S'mores

Chocolate-covered Fruits

Brownie Bites

Pecan-glazed Pineapple Bites

Caramel Banana Bites

This station can be attended by a cook or chef making lollipops in front of guests; or it can be set up as a display buffet table only. The menu can be savory or sweet. For the latter, lollipop sticks, bite-size food or pastry items and garnish, can be displayed in long ceramic pots filled with Styrofoam™, for customers to grab, or a drilled Plexiglas™ display.

Buffet of Small Plates and Glasses

MINIATURE VERSIONS OF FIRST PLATES

Sea Scallops, Truffle Pea Coulis

Seared Salmon with Mango Sorbet

Lobster Club on Vanilla Brioche

Warm Candied Tomatoes with Ricotta Sorbet

Foie Gras Terrine, Muscat Jelly

MINIATURE GLASSES FILLED WITH FLAVOR

Cold Butternut Soup, Maple Pecan Cream

Jellied Lobster Consommé

Potato Truffle Mousse with Quail Egg

Tomato Water with Basil Oil

Cantaloupe Frappé, Pecan Salt

For this station, you can serve a variety of two-bite treats either on 2/3-inch (1.5-cm) plates or in 2/3-ounce (15-ml) different-shaped glasses. Provide a wooden tray or Bento box for customers to carry their selections.

ACCENTUATING IDEAS

It is often the little things that can mean the difference between success and failure of a buffet—for example, a flavor accent that complements the various dishes on the buffet. On individual buffet stations, adding small, creative touches can make the overall presentation look all the more appealing, exciting and impressing guests as they walk into the room. And when they approach more closely, they will see and appreciate the hard work and attention to detail given to every aspect of the buffet, adding to their enjoyment of the food and the experience.

The following sequence of photos shows samples of some of the well-thought-out details that can be used to accentuate the items on a buffet and that come together in a big picture to provide the all-important wow factor.

Edible flowers, used in moderation, can enhance the look of any salad.

The way the ham is rolled, the very thin layer of white fat, even the way the bread is toasted and the tomato relish is spread, make for a canapé guests cannot wait to sink their teeth into.

On this simple display of pastry parfaits, the selections are offered in smaller portions to entice guests to try many different options.

Center stage here are the food vessels, which can really make a difference in the style of service and overall look. On this omelet bar, the slim oval bowls look elegant, yet are practical—the cook can easily reach the fillings while making the omelets.

Using space efficiently is crucial to handling customer volume and ensuring a great-looking buffet. At this made-to-order omelet bar, guests can browse other breakfast fare while waiting for their omelets.

At this simple savory martini bar, a selection of dishes, which feature starch as the main component, are topped off with a braised or roasted protein and served in martini glasses. The lighting from the heat lamps adds a dramatic effect. The result: A wow factor for the guest and a concept you can upsell to clients at a food cost that ensures profit.

Everyone loves cookies, and what better way to present them than as delicious decorations on this holiday tree. Prior to baking, a very small round cutter was used to punch a hole in the dough; once baked and cooled, ribbon was inserted through the holes for hanging. A perfect example of how a buffet item can double as decoration.

From the Chef's Pantry

The recipes presented here are intended to be used as guidelines—blueprints—for your own creativity and progress. Following are those recipes referenced in the chapters of this book.

In addition, you'll find a collection of additional items you can use to infuse flavor, finish a dish, or enhance the items on your buffet on this book's companion web site (www.wiley.com/college/leonard).

Avocado Mayonnaise | YIELD: 3 CUPS (710 ML)

INGREDIENTS

3 Pasteurized egg yolks	2 tbsp / 30 ml Lime juice, fresh
1 tsp / 5 ml Kosher salt	1 Hass avocado, very ripe
1 pinch White pepper	1–1/2 cups / 375 ml Olive oil

Method

1. Place the egg yolks, salt, pepper, and lime juice into a food processor bowl.

2. Cut the avocado in half and remove the pit and outer skin; add the avocado to the food processor.

3. Turn on the food processor to high speed and purée the mixture until silky smooth.

4. Reduce speed of food processor to medium; slowly add the oil until combined into a homogenous mixture.

5. Season to taste with salt and pepper. Reserve covered in the refrigerator for service. Use within 2 days.

Basic Buttercream | YIELD: 5–7 CUPS (1.25–1.75 L)

INGREDIENTS

1 Large egg

5 Large egg yolks

2 cups / 450 ml Sugar

1/3 cup / 80 ml Water

1–1/2 lb / 675 g Unsalted butter, room temperature

6 tbsp / 90 ml Vanilla extract

Method

1. Place egg and yolks in mixer with whisk attachment; beat at medium speed until pale yellow.

2. In medium saucepan, combine sugar and water; mix with wooden spoon until sugar is dissolved. Using a wet, clean pastry brush, wash down the sides of the pan to prevent crystallization. Without stirring, boil mixture until it reaches 240°F (115°C).

3. With mixer on medium speed, slowly pour the sugar mixture in a very thin stream near the edge of the bowl. Crucial: If you pour too fast, you end up with scrambled eggs. Mix 10–15 minutes until outside of the bowl is just warm to the touch.

4. Add butter in pieces, one at a time. The mixture may break and begin to separate; keep the mixer running and continue to add butter until it begins to smooth out. Add vanilla or any flavorings.

Coffee Buttercream | YIELD: 6 CUPS (1125 ml)

INGREDIENTS

1X Basic Buttercream (above), about 5 cups (1125 ml)

2 oz / 60 g Bittersweet chocolate, melted and cooled to room temperature

1–1/2 tbsp / 20 ml Espresso powder

2 tbsp / 30 ml Coffee liqueur

Method

1. In large mixing bowl, on medium-low speed blend 1/2 cup (120 ml) basic buttercream into melted chocolate.

2. Stir in espresso powder; add mixture to remaining buttercream filling.

3. Blend in liqueur and mix for 1 minute.

Hazelnut Buttercream | YIELD: 5–7 CUPS (1.25–1.75 L)

INGREDIENTS

1X   Basic Buttercream (p. 193), about 5 cups (1125 ml), room temperature

to taste   Hazelnut liqueur/hazelnut paste

1 cup / 225 ml   Hazelnuts, toasted and chopped, for texture (optional)

Method

1. Mix basic buttercream on medium-low speed until smooth. Using a small propane torch, you may need to lightly torch the sides of bowl to emulsify the icing, being careful not to let it get too soft and loose.

2. Once correct consistency has been reached, gently fold liqueur or nut paste into 1 cup (225 ml) of buttercream. Fold this mixture into remaining buttercream. Depending on strength of nut paste, add 1 tsp (5 ml) at a time until desirable flavor.

Béarnaise Sauce | YIELD: 1 CUP (225 ML)

Rich decadent and full of flavor, Béarnaise sauce can be used for meats, variations of eggs Benedict, and grilled seafood such as swordfish.

INGREDIENTS

1 cup / 225 ml   Butter, unsalted

3   Egg yolks

1 tsp / 5 ml   Tarragon vinegar

1 tsp / 5 ml   Lemon juice, fresh

1 tsp / 5 ml   Tarragon, chopped

as needed   Kosher salt

as needed   Tabasco

Method

1. Slowly heat the butter in a heavy saucepan until hot and foamy but not browned. Ladle off the clear butter and place into a container and reserve; discard the remaining butter solids.

2. In a small, stainless-steel bowl, whisk the egg yolks with the vinegar and lemon juice until foamy.

3. Place the bowl over a pan of low-simmering water and whisk constantly until the egg mixture begins to thicken and doubles in volume. Do not let the mixture get too hot, or the eggs will scramble.

4. Remove bowl from heat; slowly add clear butter, while whisking constantly until all butter is incorporated.

5. Add chopped tarragon and whisk to incorporate. Season béarnaise to taste with salt and Tabasco.

6. Use immediately or reserve covered in a warm place until needed.

Braised Beef Short Ribs I SERVES 8

INGREDIENTS

8 Short rib portions, 4–6 in. (10–15 cm) long	1–1/2 qt / 1.5 L Veal stock
3 tbsp / 45 ml Olive oil	1 Bouquet garni
3 tbsp / 45 ml Butter	3 cloves Garlic, sliced
1 Onion, diced	1/4 cup / 60 g Carrot, brunoise-cut
2 Carrots, diced	1/4 cup / 60 g Onion, brunoise-cut
1/2 cup / 120 ml Cremini mushrooms, quartered	1/4 cup / 60 g Celery, brunoise-cut
3 Celery stalks, diced	2 tbsp / 30 ml All-purpose flour
1/2 cup / 120 ml Tomato paste	1/2 cup / 120 g Roma tomatoes, peeled, seeded, and diced
2 cups / 450 ml Red wine	as needed Kosher salt
1/4 cup / 60 ml Balsamic vinegar	as needed Fresh cracked pepper

Everyone loves braised short ribs, slow-cooked meat that absorbs all the aromatics and flavors of the broth it cooks in. For buffet service, short ribs hold well, are customer favorites, and can be used in breakfast, lunch, and dinner preparations.

Method

1. Preheat oven to 450°F (230°C). Trim the short ribs, if needed, and pat dry with paper towel. Season with salt and pepper.

2. Place the seasoned ribs onto a sheet pan with a roasting rack and sear in the oven for 12–15 minutes, to brown and remove fat. Remove from the oven and reserve.

3. Heat a 6-qt (6-L) heavy-bottom braising pan over medium heat. Add 2 tbsp (30 ml) olive oil and 2 tbsp (30 ml) butter.

4. Add the diced onions, carrots, mushrooms, and celery. Cook, stirring occasionally, until vegetables are golden brown. Add tomato paste and continue to cook, stirring often, for 5 minutes.

5. Deglaze with the wine and vinegar and continue to cook until most of the liquid is reduced.

6. Place the ribs into the pan, along with the veal stock and bouquet garni. Cover tightly and place the pan into a preheated 275°F (135°C) oven; cook until the ribs are tender, approximately 3–4 hours.

7. Remove the pan from the oven and the short ribs from the pan. Reserve.

8. Strain the liquid through a fine sieve into a saucepan. Bring to a simmer and allow to cook for 20 minutes. Remove from the heat and reserve.

9. In clean saucepan, heat 1 tbsp (15 ml) olive oil and 1 tbsp (15 ml) butter over medium heat. Add sliced garlic and brunoise vegetables; cook until tender. Add flour and mix well; continue to cook for 3 minutes.

10. Add diced tomatoes and reserved cooking liquid from ribs. Bring to a boil then reduce to a simmer; simmer 10 minutes. Season liquid to taste with salt and pepper. Reserve for service with cooked short ribs.

Candied Leeks | YIELD: APPROXIMATELY 10 PORTIONS

INGREDIENTS

- 1 Leek
- 1 Simple Syrup (p. 204)

Method

1. Cut off the root end of the leek.

2. Slice into two long strips, 1-in. × 1/2-in. (2.5-cm × 1.25-cm) wide.

3. Gently warm the simple syrup and then dip slices into the syrup. Remove.

4. Place strips on Silpat® and dry in a 225°F (105°C) oven for 3 hours. Remove from oven; the leeks will crisp up as they cool.

Clarified Butter | YIELD: 1 CUP (225 ML)

INGREDIENTS

- 1 lb / 450 g   Unsalted butter

Method

1. Heat the butter in a heavy-bottom 2-qt (2-L) stainless-steel saucepan over medium-high heat until just melted.

2. Reduce heat to low and continue cooking butter for 5 minutes, until a layer of clear golden liquid (the clarified butter or butterfat) has developed between the foam on top and the milk solids and milky water that have separated from the butter. These will settle on the bottom of the pan.

3. Remove the pan from the heat; using a spoon or ladle, skim and discard the foam.

4. Ladle the clarified butter into a clean pan or large glass cup; do not include any of the milk solids that have settled to the bottom.

5. Discard the milk solids and water.

Court Bouillon | YIELD: 1 GAL (4 L)

INGREDIENTS

4 qt / 4 L	Water	2	Celery stalks
1 cup / 225 ml	White wine	1 head	Fennel
3	Limes, cut in half	3 sprigs	Parsley, fresh
2 tbsp / 30 ml	Coarse sea salt	2 sprigs	Thyme, fresh
1 tbsp / 15 ml	Black peppercorns	2	Bay leaves, fresh
2	Carrots, peeled	1 tbsp / 15 ml	Old Bay seasoning
1	Onion, peeled		

Method

1. Place water and wine into stainless-steel saucepan, squeeze in lime juice; add lime halves, salt, and pepper.

2. Coarsely chop vegetables and add to liquid, with the parsley, thyme, bay leaves, and seasoning. Bring to a boil; reduce heat and simmer for 15 minutes. Use to poach foods as directed in the recipes.

Foie Gras Torchon | YIELD: 20 1-OZ (30-G) PORTIONS

INGREDIENTS

2 lb / 900 g	Foie gras lobe	as needed	Pepper
1 bottle	Madeira	1	Truffle, medium size
as needed	Salt	2 oz / 60 ml	Truffle juice

This is the essential item for the Peanut Butter, Jelly, and Foie Gras Sandwich (p. 97)—and much more.

Method

1. Clean foie gras by removing all blood vessels (try to keep lobe intact).

2. Marinate foie gras in Madeira in a stainless-steel bowl; let rest 40 minutes at room temperature. Remove from Madeira and pat dry. Season with salt and pepper.

3. Place in 375°F (190°C) oven for 4 minutes; remove and set on a cool tray. Save melted fat for other uses.

4. Slice foie gras into 1-in. (2.5-cm) thick slabs. Slice truffle very thin with truffle slicer. Arrange foie gras in a line on a large sheet of Saran™ Wrap laid flush on countertop, followed by a layer of truffle slices. Season with salt and pepper; drizzle truffle juice over (or use fresh Madeira).

5. Place a foie gras slice atop the truffle (creating a truffle "sandwich"). Wrap torchon with Saran™ Wrap and tie with string. Prick torchon with a needle to squeeze out excess fat. Chill until ready to serve.

Frangipane | SERVES 8

INGREDIENTS

2 lb 3 oz / 1 kg Almond paste	1 lb 1/12 oz / 495 g Butter, soft
1 lb 1–1/2 oz / 495 g Whole eggs	2–1/2 oz / 75 g Cake flour

Frangipane is a basic batter for many tart shells and petite fours. It is moist and flavorful, making it perfect for buffet service items.

Method

1. Place the almond paste in a bowl; using a paddle, soften by adding small amounts of egg at a time.

2. Add the soft butter to the almond paste mixture. Scrape down bowl well.

3. Cream the almond paste and butter until light and fluffy. Fold in sifted flour.

4. Spread on baking sheet.

5. Bake at 325°F (165°C) for 20 minutes, or until firm.

Hazelnut Cake | SERVES 8

INGREDIENTS

2–1/2 lb / 1.1 kg Butter	15 oz / 420 g Cake flour
2–1/2 lb / 1.1 kg Granulated sugar	2–1/2 lbs / 1.1 kg Hazelnut flour
15 Whole eggs	

A rich cake full of hazelnut flavor, it pairs well with chocolate- or nutella-type fillings for an incredible taste.

Method

1. Place the butter and sugar in a bowl; cream until smooth.

2. Add eggs slowly, scraping down the mixing bowl.

3. Sift flours together and incorporate to butter mixture. Scrape down bowl.

4. Spread on baking sheet. Bake at 350°F (175°C) for 25 minutes, or until done.

Hollandaise Sauce | YIELD: 1 CUP (225 ML)

INGREDIENTS

1/2 cup / 120 ml Clarified Butter (p. 196)	1/2 tsp / 2 ml White vinegar
4 Egg yolks	to taste Cayenne pepper
1 tbsp / 15 ml Freshly squeezed lemon juice	to taste Kosher salt

Method

1. Melt butter in a small stainless-steel saucepan over medium heat.

2. Vigorously whisk the egg yolks, lemon juice, and vinegar together in a clean and dry stainless-steel bowl, until the mixture is thickened to a ribbon-like consistency.

3. Place the bowl over a saucepan of barely simmering water; make sure the bowl does not touch the pan.

4. Continue to whisk rapidly using a full motion. Do not let the eggs get too hot, or they will scramble; the key is low heat and a fast whisking movement.

5. Slowly drizzle in the clarified butter and continue to whisk until sauce is thickened and doubled in volume.

6. Remove from heat. Whisk in pepper and salt to taste; for a nice twist, add a dash of chipotle hot sauce.

7. Cover and place in a warm spot until ready to use. If sauce gets too thick, whisk in a few drops of warm water before serving.

Tomato Hollandaise Preparation

1. For every 1 cup (225 ml) Hollandaise Sauce, whisk in 2 tbsp (30 ml) warm, strained tomato sauce.

> One of the mother sauces that is still a customer favorite. There are many variations that can be created from this rich foundation sauce.

Italian Meringue | SERVES 8

INGREDIENTS

1 lb / 450 g	Granulated sugar	8 oz / 225 g	Egg whites
4 oz / 115 g	Water		

One of three meringue types, this has a sweet, marshmallow-like consistency. It is great for cakes, tarts, and frozen desserts.

Method

1. Place the sugar and water in a pot. Cook to 240°F (115°C).

2. Place the egg whites in a bowl and whip until they form soft peaks.

3. When the sugar has reached the correct temperature, add it in a slow, steady stream to the egg whites. Whip until thick in consistency.

4. Use immediately.

Ketchup | YIELD: 2 CUPS (450 ML)

INGREDIENTS

Try making ketchup for your own signature touch for burgers, fries, and other items on the buffet. It's a vast improvement over bottled or canned varieties.

2 lbs / 900 g	Overripe tomatoes, peeled, diced	1/2 cup / 125 ml	Cider vinegar
2	Medium onions, diced	1/2 tsp / 2 ml	Kosher salt
3	Garlic cloves	1 tsp / 5 ml	Celery salt
1	Carrot, peeled and diced	1	Cinnamon stick
6 tbsp / 60 ml	Olive oil	1/2	Vanilla bean
6 tbsp / 60 ml	Tomato paste	1/2 tsp / 2 ml	Allspice
2/3 cup / 160 ml	Dark brown sugar	5	Cloves

Method

1. In a heavy-bottom pan, sauté onion, carrots, and garlic in oil until well caramelized.

2. Add tomato paste and sugar; cook 2–3 minutes.

3. Deglaze the pan with vinegar; add tomatoes and remaining items. Cook for 2–3 hours on slow heat, or in a 260°F (125°C) oven, until rich and thick. Press through a sieve or chinois.

Lobster Mousse | YIELD: 1–1/2 QT (1.125 L)

INGREDIENTS

1 gal / 4 L	Court Bouillon (p. 197)
3	Lobsters (1–1/4 lb each)
3 oz / 85 g	Halibut fillet, cleaned
4 oz / 115 g	Scallop, cleaned
1	Egg, cracked

1–1/2 tsp / 7 ml	Brandy
4 oz / 115 g	Heavy cream
1 tbsp / 15 ml	Fresh dill, chopped
as needed	Kosher salt
as needed	Fresh cracked black pepper

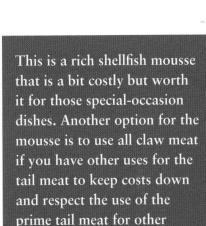

Method

1. Place 1 gal (4 L) of court bouillon over high heat and bring to a boil.

2. Remove the tail and claws from the lobsters. Reserve the carapace for later use.

3. Add lobster claws to boiling court bouillon; after 30 seconds add lobster tails. Continue to cook 1 minute. Remove the lobster from the court bouillon and place into an ice water bath.

4. Remove lobster meat from shells; remove all cartilage from the meat. Reserve shells for later use.

5. Place the cleaned lobster meat into a food processor and process on high for about 4 minutes, or until the lobster becomes a brilliant red color. Add the halibut and scallop to the lobster meat and process on high for 1 minute.

6. While the food processor is running, slowly add the egg and then the brandy. Slowly add the heavy cream until all is absorbed into the mousse.

7. Remove the mousse from the food processor and place into a stainless-steel bowl that is positioned on top of a second stainless-steel bowl full of ice. Fold in the chopped dill, and season to taste with salt and pepper.

8. Reserve the lobster mousse, covered, in the refrigerator until ready to serve.

This is a rich shellfish mousse that is a bit costly but worth it for those special-occasion dishes. Another option for the mousse is to use all claw meat if you have other uses for the tail meat to keep costs down and respect the use of the prime tail meat for other menu items.

Mango Gelée | SERVES 8

INGREDIENTS

1 lb / 450 g	Mango purée
5	Gelatin sheets

A gelée to coat individual pastries and tarts.

Method

1. Heat the purée to a boil.

2. Cool to 140°F (60°C).

3. To bloom the gelatin, place the sheets into very cold water for 5 minutes; remove and squeeze dry.

4. Add the bloomed gelatin to the mango purée and mix gently to combine. Store in refrigerator.

5. To use, heat in microwave until liquid. Do not overheat.

Olive Oil Tomato Petals | YIELD: 16 PETALS

INGREDIENTS

4	Plum tomatoes, peel, quartered, and deseeded	1 tsp / 5 ml	Sugar
2 cloves	Garlic, thinly sliced	2 tsp / 10 ml	Kosher salt
1/2 cup / 125 ml	Extra-virgin olive oil	1 tsp / 5 ml	Crushed red pepper flakes
		to cover	Extra-virgin olive oil

Here's a flavorful way to showcase tomatoes on their own, as a side dish for main plates, or as an addition to salads and on buffet action stations

Method

1. Place the tomato petals in a bowl; gently toss with garlic, olive oil, sugar, salt, and red pepper flakes.

2. Spread the mixture evenly in a small baking pan. Cover with olive oil.

3. Place in a 160°F (70°C) oven for 6–8 hours.

4. Carefully remove the tomato petals from the oil, wrap tightly, and refrigerate until ready to use. Use warm or at room temperature.

5. Refrigerate oil for other uses.

Oven-Dried Grape Tomatoes | YIELD: 8

INGREDIENTS

8 Red or yellow grape tomatoes	as needed Kosher salt
1 tbsp / 15 ml Extra-virgin olive oil	as needed Fresh cracked pepper
dash Balsamic vinegar	

Method

1. In a stainless-steel bowl, combine the tomatoes, oil, and vinegar. Season lightly with salt and pepper; toss to coat the tomatoes evenly.

2. Place the seasoned tomatoes onto a half sheet pan with a roasting rack, and place into a preheated 180°F (80°C) oven and allow the tomatoes to dry for 6–8 hours.

3. Remove from the oven and reserve for service.

Sweet grape tomatoes take on a new twist by drying them in an oven; they make for great buffet dish garnishes or for salads.

Signature Vegetable Crust | YIELD: 2 CUPS (450 ML)

INGREDIENTS

1 Zucchini	1 Eggplant
1 Yellow squash	4 sprigs Fresh thyme
1 Carrot, peeled	1 sprig Fresh rosemary
1 Yellow carrot, peeled	6 Fresh sage leaves
1 Portobello mushroom	

Dehydrators in kitchens are becoming commonplace equipment. This crust takes advantage of drying out fresh vegetables for a very colorful and flavorful crust for fish.

Method

1. Remove the ends from the zucchini, yellow squash, carrots, and eggplant. Using either a mandoline or an electric slicer, slice all vegetables into 1/16-inch (1-mm) thick slices.

2. Place all the vegetable slices and herbs into a food dehydrator. Turn the dehydrator on medium heat and allow the vegetables and herbs to dry completely, approximately 6–10 hours.

3. Transfer all the vegetables from the dehydrator to a food processor. Pulse the dried vegetables gently, until they are broken down into small flakes.

4. Remove the vegetable flakes from the food processor. Store in an airtight container for up to 1 month.

Simple Syrup | YIELD: 3 CUPS (700 ML)

INGREDIENTS

2 cups / 500 ml Water	1 Cinnamon stick
2 cup / 500 ml Sugar	1 Vanilla bean, split
4 Cloves	

This syrup can be infused to create many different flavor profiles, with ingredients such as fresh herbs, fruit rinds, vanilla bean, star anise, cloves, and more.

Method

1. Combine all ingredients in a stainless-steel saucepan and boil for 5 minutes.

2. Strain and cool.

Spiced Tomato Jam | YIELD: 4 CUPS (1 L)

INGREDIENTS

3 cups / 675 ml Tomatoes, peeled, seeded	1/4 tsp / 1 ml Ground cloves
1–1/2 tsp / 7 ml Lime zest, grated	3–1/2 cups / 800 ml Granulated sugar
1/2 tsp / 2 ml Ground allspice	1 cup / 225 ml Light brown sugar
1/8 tsp / 1/2 ml Red pepper flakes	1/8 tsp / 1/2 ml Vanilla powder
1/2 tsp / 2 ml Fresh basil, chiffonade	2–3/4 oz / 80 g Powdered pectin
1/2 tsp / 2 ml Ground cinnamon	1/4 cup / 60 ml Fresh lime juice

Tomatoes are one of the most diverse fruits and to learn about them is a long-time study. This jam just shows another use for such an item that people consider a kitchen staple. For grilled meats, poultry, and vegetarian dishes this jams adds a flavor hit.

Method

1. In a stainless-steel saucepan, place the tomatoes, lime zest, allspice, pepper flakes, basil, cinnamon, cloves, vanilla powder, and lime juice.

2. Add the powdered pectin and bring to a boil over high heat, stirring constantly.

3. All at once, stir in sugar. While stirring, bring to a full rolling boil that cannot be stirred down.

4. Continue to boil hard for 1 minute. Remove from heat and skim off foam.

5. Pour hot jam immediately into a shallow pan. Allow to cool completely in the refrigerator before using.

6. Store covered for up to 1 month.

Tart Dough | SERVES 8

INGREDIENTS

1–1/2 lb / 675 g Butter	3 Eggs
12 oz / 340 g Granulated sugar	2 lb 4 oz / 1 kg All-purpose flour

Method

1. Place butter and sugar in bowl of 5-quart (5-L) mixer. Using a paddle, mix on medium speed until smooth; scrape down bowl. Add eggs, in stages; scrape down sides of bowl.

2. Sift the flour; incorporate into mixture. Mix until smooth.

3. Place dough in refrigerator covered with plastic wrap until ready to use.

Tart Shell Preparation

1. Sheet or roll chilled tart dough to 1/6 in. (1 mm) thickness. Transfer dough to fluted tart pan. Use floured scrap dough to press corners of dough firmly against bottom and sides of pan.

2. Dock unbaked tart shell; line with foil and fill with baking beans. Blind-bake approximately 12 minutes, or until edges turn light golden brown. Remove beans and foil and finish baking; bottom will turn golden brown.

3. Fill shell and finish in oven according to filling instructions; or chill.

> A good, basic tart dough for a variety of pastry items.

Waffles | YIELD: 4 TO 6 WAFFLES

INGREDIENTS

2 cups / 450 ml All-purpose flour	1 tsp / 5 ml Olive oil
1 tsp / 5 ml Kosher salt	1–1/2 cups / 375 ml Buttermilk, warm
4 tsp / 20 ml Baking powder	1/3 cup / 150 ml Butter, melted
2 tbsp / 30 ml Sugar	1 tsp / 5 ml Real vanilla
2 Eggs	

Method

1. In a large bowl, mix together flour, salt, baking powder, and sugar; set aside.

2. Preheat waffle iron to desired temperature.

3. In a separate bowl, whisk eggs with oil. Stir in buttermilk, butter, and vanilla. Pour mixture into flour mixture; mix well until blended. Ladle batter into waffle iron. Cook waffles until golden and crisp on the outside.

> A family favorite and great addition to buffets as a breakfast sandwich item or an action station with a variety of toppings or just simply done and topped with butter and real maple syrup.

Where to Buy What You See

The centerpiece of any buffet is, of course, the food. But integral to the enjoyment of that food is how it is presented. Below you'll find sources for buffet supplies you have seen in the photos throughout this book, to showcase the many buffets described, and I highly recommend them to you.

GLASSWARE DESIGN AND CUSTOM ITEMS

Seagull Glass Works & Bobby Castillo
www.seagullglass.com.ph

In the United States
All Things Culinary Group
Phone: 203–517–5626
Email: chefsmenucentral@aol.com

In Asia
4186 Ponte St.
Makati City
1204 Philippines
Phone: (632) 897–4036 / 896–9903 / 897–3740
Fax: (632) 897–4017 / 897–4038
Email: seagullglass@globelines.com.ph, info@seagullglass.com.ph

CHINA AND GLASSWARE

Fortessa, Inc. www.fortessa.com

In the United States
22601 Davis Drive
Sterling, VA 20164
Phone: (800) 296–7508
Fax: (703) 787–6645
Email: info@fortessa.com

In Europe
Tableware Enterprises GmbH
Fortessa of Europe
Sonnenstrasse 19
92681 Erbendorf
Germany
Phone: 0049 9682 915 038
Fax: 0049 9682 915 039

In Canada
Fortessa of Canada
330 Esna Park Drive, Unit 38
Markham, Ontario L3R 1H3
Canada
Phone: 905–470–0646
Fax: 905–470–6314

CONTEMPORARY TABLES AND DESIGN

Southern Aluminum
www.southernaluminum.com

5 Hwy. 82 West; PO Box 884
Magnolia, AR 71754
Phone: (800) 221–0408 / (870) 234–8660
Fax: (870) 234–2823
Email: sales@southernaluminum.com

CHEF TOOLS, KNIFES, BOOKS, AND GARDE ITEMS

Fortessa, Inc.

JB Prince
36 East 31st Street
New York, NY 10016
Phone: (800) 473–0577 / (212) 683–3553
www.jbprince.com

Chef Revival & San Jamar
555 Koopman Lane
Elkhorn, Wisconsin 53121 USA
Phone: 262-723-6133
Fax: 262-723-4204
Customer Care: 800-248-9826
CustomerCare@sanjamar.com
www.chefrevival.com
www.katchall.com

INDEX